IN SEARCH OF

THE LOST ARK OF THE COVENANT

IN SEARCH OF

THE LOST ARK OF THE COVENANT

ROBERT CORNUKE
AND
DAVID HALBROOK

BROADMAN
& HOLMAN
PUBLISHERS

Nashville, Tennessee

Published by Broadman & Holman Publishers,
Nashville, Tennessee

Dewey Decimal Classification: 221
Subject Heading: BIBLE

1 2 3 4 5 6 7 8 9 10 06 05 04 03 02

Contents

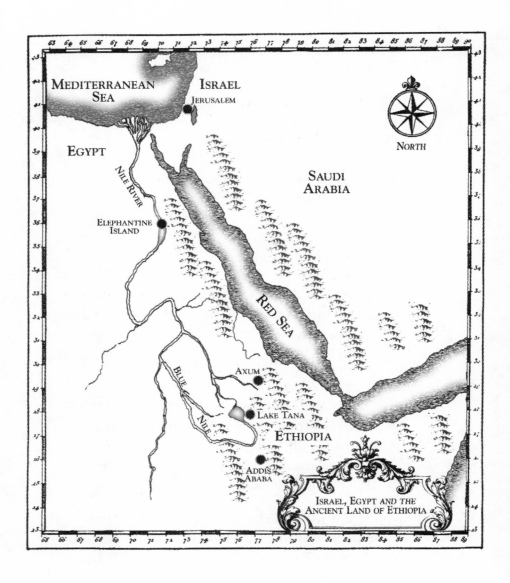

Introduction

IN SEARCH OF FORGOTTEN PATHS

The town of Axum—if it can even be called a town—lies in the rugged, dust-dry highlands of north-central Ethiopia. Once the center of a powerful kingdom rivaling the mightiest nations of the ancient past, Axum today is little more than a dusty village decaying into obscurity. Lying some 350 miles inland from the Red Sea coast, it looks little different from dozens of other mud-hut villages strewn across Ethiopia's rugged Abyssinian Highlands.

Yet Axum is different.

At the center of town sits a simple daub chapel. This thick-walled shrine, known as the Chapel of Saint Mary of Zion, stands as the most venerated of the country's more than twenty thousand churches and monasteries. Strange as it may seem, this humble structure lays claim to perhaps the greatest secret in history. Within its rude walls may sit an object whose nature, appearance, and fate have puzzled and fascinated man since the days of Moses—the original ark of the covenant!

THE ARK OF THE COVENANT

Words on a page fail to convey the ark's incalculable value to the Judeo-Christian world. This plum of archaeology—crafted at Mount Sinai of acacia wood, overlaid with gold, sent wandering in the wilderness, and eventually placed in Solomon's temple—not only provided a sacred repository of the Ten Commandments (the moral code of law and justice governing every civilized society since), but it also reportedly channeled the power to stop mighty rivers, lay waste to walled cities, wipe out armies, and certify kingdoms.

The Bible refers to the ark more than two hundred times, from the days of Moses to the reign of Solomon. The ark plays a prominent, even profound role in the history of early Israel. But then, for reasons that still baffle scholars and theologians, its story simply ends.

Sometime between the tenth and sixth centuries B.C., the ark of the covenant simply vanished from the Holy of Holies in the Jerusalem temple and disappeared from the pages of biblical history. Aside from a few veiled references scattered here and there, the ark simply vanished.

Yet in Ethiopia today one can hardly find a single individual out of a population of sixty million who harbors the slightest doubt that the ark lies quietly in state in the chapel at Axum. From the lowliest peasant to the highest public official, all insist that, secured within the shadows of St. Mary of Zion's fortified inner sanctum, separated from the outside world only by a high iron fence and a lonely guardian, sits a wooden chest of biblical significance.

No other city on the planet makes such a claim. The monk pledged to guard the object until the day of his death affirms that, "Yes, we do possess the sacred Tabot, that is to say the ark of the covenant." And then, perhaps to deflect further questions, he notes, "The description given in the Bible is accurate."

Join me now as we attempt to find answers to riddles cloaked in Scripture for untold millennia. Hold your breath as we peer behind the curtain to snatch a glimpse at truths perhaps veiled even to the prophets. Let us together enter that misty realm of mirrors and shadows we call Ethiopia and travel forgotten paths known only to the keepers of the ark.

PART ONE

MYSTERY IN EXOTIC ETHIOPIA

Oπε

IN THE BEGINNING

Terry and I were practically newlyweds in 1993, and the notion of spending a couple of nights in a billionaire's mansion sounded, if not deeply romantic, then at least like a cool adventure.

I vaguely knew Robert Van Kampen as a billionaire who fit the mold of an old-style, baron philanthropist. His father had amassed a fortune in brick manufacturing, and young Robert made his reputation selling bonds, eventually founding a pioneering investment firm. When he sold Van Kampen Funds to Xerox in 1984, he netted $200 million; today the company controls more than $79 billion in assets.[1]

Just before our trip I learned Van Kampen was also a devout Christian with an almost fanatical obsession with the Bible. After amassing one of the world's most extensive collections of ancient Bibles and manuscripts, he'd written a book, *The Sign*, about biblical prophecy and the end of the world. And I was about to meet him.

Our plane landed in Chicago in the icy dead of winter. Van Kampen said he'd send his private helicopter to pick us up and whisk us away to his sprawling estate on Lake Michigan's shoreline, but we learned on arrival that the chopper had been grounded with mechanical problems. So we rented a car and drove four hours through the sleet and snow to Grand Haven, Michigan, where we pulled over in the snowstorm to ask a policeman how to get to Robert Van Kampen's home.

"Oh, you mean the Monster House," the policeman declared through his frozen mustache. He pointed toward a Stonehenge-like structure peering above some snow-covered hilltops. From a distance it looked like a metal-and-glass, high-rise office building. I turned back to the cop, who nodded and said, "That's it. Keep it in sight as you cut through these hills."

We followed the icy road into a dense, snowy thicket, arriving at the entrance barred by an enormous iron gate. I walked up and pushed the intercom button.

"Hello?" said a voice.

"I'm Robert Cornuke. I'm here to see Robert Van Kampen," I said, slightly embarrassed.

Immediately the gate swung open. We drove another mile or so along a winding lane through rolling, snow-frosted forests. We passed frozen sand dunes angling sharply against Lake Michigan's barren shoreline and at length arrived at a handsome beach house perched on a crusty knoll overlooking the shore. From the car we could see tall, dead stands of brown Indian grass and bushy pines shivering under the bitter lakefront wind.

We wrapped up tight and skittered to the front door, where Van Kampen himself invited us in. His wife, Judy, joined us in the warm portico and tossed our coats casually on a bench. "Bless your hearts," she said, "you must be freezing."

The home looked elegant though not extravagant. A heavy Victorian-style pool table sat under a hanging wrought-iron lamp in the den. A massive stone fireplace dominated the grand room, accented with nicely appointed furniture. Knowing our hosts ranked high on the short list of global billionaires, I craned my neck, hoping to see Chauncy the butler or a team of French maids arriving with drinks and hors d'oeuvres. But we saw no waiters, no doormen, no attendants— just the Van Kampens, looking casually at home in their wool sweaters and slippers.

Judy struck us immediately as the motherly type, plying us with questions, setting us at ease. Van Kampen, however, made no such overtures. Bespeckled, stocky, middle-aged, he maintained a courteous yet stoic gruffness throughout our stay. Years of risk-taking at the highest levels had honed his personality to a cold, razor edge, teaching him to dispense with formalities and cut to the chase. Time is money, after all; and I got the feeling that, if it weren't for his wife, he would've quickly dragged me aside and started grilling me with questions.

But dinner awaited, and we sat down to a modest buffet of broiled chicken and vegetables, which Judy herself—not a wait staff—served in stages. Judy seemed kind and sweet, a delightful hostess unwilling to put on airs.

After coffee, Van Kampen waived us into the living room, where we sat facing our hosts. They seated themselves in a wooden porch swing near the fireplace, suspended from the ceiling. "We like to swing after dinner, to relax," Judy said. To which her husband bluntly added, "We don't like to have conversations with anybody unless it pertains to the Bible, and I hear you used the Bible to find Mount Sinai and then searched for Noah's ark with Apollo 15 astronaut Jim Irwin. From what I've heard, you're one of the best in your field."

I felt embarrassed and quickly switched topics, asking him about his vast Bible collection. I heard he'd collected some five thousand items, ranging from clay tablets to ancient Hebrew scrolls.

"Would you mind showing me one of your Bibles?" I asked, measuring his response. He smiled, thought for a moment, then said, "I don't see why not." He strolled from the room and returned a few minutes later, carrying a big, leather-bound Bible held together with metal hinges as from a castle door. The ornate binding had a medieval look and texture. Handing it carefully to me, he said, "I had this Bible made up specially. It contains the Book of Daniel from an original Gutenberg Bible."

I nearly gasped. If it had indeed been printed on the Gutenberg Press, I now held one of the oldest printed manuscripts in history. Terry innocently began thumbing through the pages, oblivious to its priceless pedigree. "Oh, how interesting," she said. "These pages feel so . . . *old.*"

I saw Van Kampen stiffen. "You might want to be a little more careful with those," he said. "Each page is worth well over $30,000."

"*No!*" Terry shot back, feeling feisty. "Do you mind if I have *this* one?" She took a playful swipe at the page, pretending to rip it out. As she stood there grinning, I winced.

Van Kampen smiled gamely, then calmly closed the Bible. "It's late," he said. "Let's continue our conversation in the morning."

As we said goodnight, Judy showed us to the guest bedroom at the far end of the house. It had been a long, intense day. In the quilted comfort of a king-sized bed, we immediately dropped off to sleep. Yet sometime during the night, I became vaguely aware that Terry had gone to the bathroom. By the time I sank back to sleep, she bolted into bed and yanked the covers over her head. I felt her sharp elbow in my back, then her finger pointing to my side of the bed. I rolled over to see the huge, black form of a Rottweiler, head as big as an ice chest, staring at me with black, marble eyes. Flexed menacingly just inches from my face, he sniffed the blankets suspiciously, uttering a low, malevolent growl through loose, slobbering jowls.

"You forgot to close the bedroom door!" Terry whispered angrily. "Get out there and *do* something!"

I lay silently, listening to the dog's heavy breath, imagining that even to blink might set him off.

"No way!" I whispered back. "That thing's as big as a rhinoceros. We'll just have to wait it out until morning."

We pulled the covers over our heads and held our breaths as the dog pawed about the room, sniffing at our luggage and salivating on our shoes. After what seemed like hours, we finally fell asleep. Morning came without further incident; we dressed quickly and, looking both ways in the hallway for the beast, made our escape for a quick breakfast.

Immediately afterward, leaving our wives chatting in the breakfast nook, Van Kampen and I retired to his personal office overlooking frozen Lake Michigan. Without further ado, he began interrogating me. Though he seemed fascinated and fully engaged throughout our discussion, he nonetheless kept up a distracting ritual. Every few minutes he'd nonchalantly swivel in his chair, roll back, and begin tapping keys on his widescreen computer. He'd punch the keyboard, mumble to himself—"*It's up*," or, "*It's down.*" He'd tap some more, then roll back to pick up our conversation in mid-sentence. I found it amusing to watch him buy and sell stocks—perhaps taking over whole corporations?—while carrying on an in-depth conversation. He couldn't seem to divert his attention from his computer for more than a few moments. I gained a mental picture of Van Kampen chained to his assets.

Finally, he looked at me hard and asked, "Would you consider heading up my ministry?" I hadn't expected the question, and I must have looked confused, for he added, "I'm talking about my collection of manuscripts and Bibles. I'd like you to oversee it all."

My mouth went dry. His collection was recognized interna-tionally as one of the world's great biblical research resources, with the potential of becoming one of the planet's best private research libraries for theological scholarship. I understood well the prestige connected with such a position, yet his offer left me dumbstruck. Something didn't *feel* right. After an extended pause, all I could offer was a simple, "Thank you. I'm honored to be considered for such a position, but I'll have to give it some serious consideration."

Van Kampen glared at me, as if to say, "How dare you triv-ialize my offer by saying you'll have to think about it!" He clearly hadn't been prepared for my lukewarm reply, yet he con-tinued to press his sales pitch: "Lots of other important biblical artifacts around the world are just waiting to be found," he added, "and I can see that you're the man to do it." He cleared his throat, paused, then asked, "So please explain to me— what's there to *think* about?"

I smiled, understanding how he'd sold so many mutual funds. "Mr. Van Kampen," I sighed, "it's an attractive offer, and aspects of the job genuinely appeal to me. But I'll need to go home, discuss it with Terry, and take a few weeks to give you an answer."

He shrugged, content that he'd made his best pitch. We joined our wives in the dining room, and after lunch we all bundled up and took an afternoon drive up an old, icy path leading to the Monster House. On the way we passed his ten-nis court, covered with snow. We trudged to a short flight of steps angling down beneath the court to an underground vault. The vault ran the length and width of the tennis court and lay cluttered with chunks of concrete, unopened boxes and spools of electrical wire.

"It is almost finished," he said. "It will be my Scriptorium, where I'll keep my collections." Beholding this research vault beneath the tennis court, I thought, *Only a consummate businessman would think to stretch a buck in this manner.* Passing his hand in an arc before us, he predicted, "Scholars from all over the world will travel here to study the manuscripts and scrolls."

Back outside again, we continued up the hillside to the towering dream house under construction. It loomed over Lake Michigan, a huge monolith of glass and steel. By the time we stood in its broad entryway, the edifice had grown to a height and girth that dwarfed any concept of "home." I found the sweeping scale and industrial feel of the decor unsettling. Its cold steel girders and mirrored glass reminded me of a Chicago bank building, and its sterile, glazed floors felt more like the inside of a hotel lobby than someone's home.

We rode an elevator to a top floor and found ourselves bathed in shafts of dancing light, pouring in from huge cathedral-like windows. Outside the snowstorm had ended, and a pale light filled the house. As Van Kampen showed us each impressive facet of his streamlined castle, I glimpsed a man ill at ease with the scale of his wealth. Beneath the tight-jawed demeanor, I imagined a soul chafing at life's endless details; suddenly I understood the freedom he felt poring over ancient manuscripts. At that moment I felt grateful for my simple life back in Colorado.

Van Kampen escorted us out of the house and across the grounds, turning back momentarily to admire his high-rise masterpiece. "I built this house so Judy and I could live out the remainder of our lives in comfort," he said. "I put the elevators in, knowing that one day I'd be too old to climb the stairs. Once we move in, that's it. I'll die there." It struck me as an odd statement.

We returned to the beach house, where Van Kampen removed his coat and strode over to a large bookcase by the fireplace. He grabbed a volume and handed it to me: *The Sign and the Seal* by Graham Hancock. Judging from the cover, it had something to do with the ark of the covenant.

13
Λ

"I'd like you to read this," he said, "and tell me what you think. I found it a fairly clever account of the search for the ark of the covenant, but given your investigative credentials, I'd like you to tell me if you think the writer is credible."

I glanced again at the cover, thumbed through some pages. "I've never heard of it," I said, "but I'd be happy to look it over." I tucked it under my arm as we said our good-byes. Within minutes Terry and I had driven back through the snowy dunes and timbers and out the front gate.

I never saw Van Kampen again. A few weeks later I called and formally declined his offer. After praying about it, Terry and I agreed that uprooting our lives in Colorado to move to Michigan didn't make sense. Informed of my decision, Van Kampen thanked me for my time and wished me well.

Van Kampen died in November 1999, at the age of sixty, waiting for a heart transplant. Not long after our trip to Grand Haven, he contracted a rare viral disease that slowly destroyed his heart. He and Judy spent the last two years of his life in the comfort of that grandiose lakefront high-rise. I pictured him content to play out his final days where he seemed always to understand he would die.

Ironically, above all else, his final request of me, made in the rushed moments before we fled Grand Haven, left a lasting imprint on my life. By asking me to read *The Sign and the Seal*, Van Kampen launched me on a wild quest. I appreciated Hancock's exhaustive research and keen detective work, if not all his speculations. In reading and re-reading his book over the next year, I came to share his fascination for the ark of the covenant. I found it provocative that this sacred object, straddling the boundary between myth and history, vanished from the pages of Scripture at about the same time it is said to have reached Ethiopian soil.

Slowly, perhaps subconsciously at first, I made mental preparations to retrace Hancock's footsteps. For reasons I had yet to define for myself, I needed to understand where the threads of truth and fiction parted ways.

Two

THE ARK OF THE PARADOX

Since the temple's primary purpose had been as a resting place for the ark, and since there can be little doubt that the ark mysteriously disappeared from the temple, it follows that any search for the ark must begin in the temple. There, cloaked in the thick darkness of the Holy of Holies, sprinkled with blood, it lay hidden until some unknown date between the tenth and sixth centuries B.C.

When *precisely* did the ark disappear? And where did it go? A belief popular among rabbis and Jewish scholars holds that it was likely taken by force during one of several military catastrophes Israel suffered after the death of Solomon. King Solomon had earned God's wrath by following the foreign gods of his thousand wives and concubines. Though Solomon escaped the consequences of his apostasy, not long after his death disaster struck Israel. The first hit came in 926 B.C., when Solomon's son, King Rehoboam, saw his kingdom overrun by the armies of Shishak, king of Egypt, who looted the temple and stole priceless treasures of gold and silver (1 Kings 14:25–26). The last saw Babylonian King

Nebuchadnezzar invade Israel in 598 B.C. and in two separate attacks penetrate deeply into the temple court (2 Kings 24:10–13), carting off all the temple treasures and destroying the bronze furnishings of the sanctuary. In between came frequent invasions, when barbarian hordes helped themselves to minor temple treasures; still, in none of the biblical accounts does the ark turn up among the spoils of war.

It is possible, of course, that the ark might have been stolen or destroyed during one of these incursions, without its disappearance ever being noted in the public record. Rank-and-file Jews never saw it anyway, and no one but the high priest ever entered the Holy of Holies to minister before the ark, and then only once a year. More likely, full disclosure of the ark's loss came much later, when Jews returning to Israel from the Babylonian exile attended the dedication of the second temple.

This temple, completed between 517 and 515 B.C. and built above the razed foundations of the first,[1] differed from the original primarily in that its sanctuary did *not* contain: the ark and the mercy seat. When it became known that the centerpiece of temple worship could not be returned to the second temple, the Hebrews must have understood the ark had not been taken to Babylon. To the horror of the returning exiles, the most precious object of the Jewish faith had simply vanished. Its disappearance could now be positively traced to the time of the first temple.

Jewish traditions offer several possibilities for how and when this might have happened. The Talmud states that the ark was "buried in its own place" by King Josiah between 640 and 609 B.C., a mere decade before the Babylonian invasion.[2] This supports the popular notion that the ark took its leave before Nebuchadnezzar's looters arrived, likely hidden by Levite priests below the Holy of Holies, deep within Mount Moriah's labyrinth of secret caverns.[3] Others believe Solomon himself, foreseeing the first temple's destruction, built these

18

caches (known collectively today as the Well of Souls) as a hiding place for the ark.

Some fringe Jewish traditions credit the ark's sudden disappearance to rescuing angels, descending just prior to the destruction of the first temple to whisk it off to heaven. Other groups believe one of the prophets, who, forewarned by God of the Babylonian invasion, buried the ark in the mountains outside Jerusalem. Second Maccabees, a work excluded from the Hebrew Bible but included in the canon of the Greek and Latin Christian churches, reports that the prophet Jeremiah stowed the ark in a cave on Mount Nebo, the same mountain Moses climbed to see the promised land. Jeremiah indeed lived at the time of the destruction of the first temple, and, say some scholars, he may have anticipated Nebuchadnezzar and concealed the ark, the tabernacle, and the altar of incense on Nebo, some thirty-five miles east of Jerusalem.[4] Another early compilation of ancient Jewish law known as The Mishnah, reports that Levite priests buried the holy relic "under the pavement of the wood house (a fuel repository for burnt offerings kept somewhere on temple grounds) so that it might not fall into the hands of the enemy."[5] Despite the provocative nature of these reports, most contemporary scholars have rejected them as thinly veiled attempts to propagandize expatriate Jews (perhaps in a post-exilic effort to fan Hebrew interest in their national homeland).

Another school of thought contends that, had the ark been hidden in or around Mount Moriah (site of both temples and the current Temple Mount), it would almost certainly have been dislodged in A.D. 70 and removed by the Romans at the razing of the second temple. From there it would have been taken to Rome with the other temple treasures and, once Christianity became the dominant religion of the Roman Empire, placed in the hands of the Catholic Church. To be sure, some purported eyewitnesses claim that it remains locked in the crypts below the Vatican.[6] Others say the ark and the temple treasures one day will be found in the recently excavated Jewish Quarter in Jerusalem, in underground vaults of the ancient Nea ("New") Church, built in the sixth century A.D. by emperor Justinian.[7]

A common thread runs through each of these scenarios: While the ark certainly disappeared and remains hidden somewhere, it was never proven to have perished. If the ark really had been destroyed, even the most liberal critics argue that the catastrophe certainly would have been noted in the Bible. Yet Scripture never even hints at such a terrible event; the ark simply ceases to be mentioned.

Still the ark continues to tantalize the imagination. Some say evidence of its significance can still be seen, and felt, in the New Testament. No less than the Book of Revelation seems to affirm the importance of the earthly ark by its clear reference to the heavenly prototype (Rev. 11:19), which, in turn, gives reason to contemplate that the ark has a future role to play in God's divine purpose. "The Ark," says Bible prophecy scholar Randall Price, "is most likely hidden in some secret location, awaiting the proper time on God's calendar to makes its reappearance."[8]

Here again, the story circles back to the ageless question: Where is the ark? The bulk of Jewish scholarship argues that the ark lies hidden somewhere within the holy city or, failing that, in Israel proper. This prejudice explains why history's most prominent ark excavations have focused on Jerusalem or on one of Israel's Old Testament landmarks. The reigning theory among rabbis maintains that the ark lies buried beneath the Dome of the Rock, probably in one of the subterranean passages honeycombing Jerusalem's Temple Mount (or the Haram al-Sharif, one of Islam's holiest places).

This theory has been almost impossible to test since the ultimate Jewish sacred site has admitted no Jewish worship since the destruction of the second temple in A.D. 70. And with the construction on the Dome of the Rock in the seventh century A.D.—effectively placing the entire Temple Mount under Islamic control—access to the site has evaporated. Even when the Six-Day War of 1967 briefly returned the Temple Mount to Israel, jurisdiction quickly reverted to the Muslims, who to this day aggressively guard the site (as well as caves and structures beneath) against outside contact.

For religious Jews—who look to the discovery of the ark as a prophetic signpost of Israel's return to splendor—it seems tragic (and a bit ironic) that, in an era of technology that might lend itself to successful exploration of the Mount, opportunities to explore do not exist. Or do they?

In 1867, a young lieutenant assigned to Britain's Royal Engineers cut a tunnel under the exterior walls of the Temple Mount in a clandestine maneuver to secure the ark. Predictably, the clamor of sledgehammers and pickaxes below the Al-Aqsa Mosque disturbed the prayers of the Muslim faithful above, triggering a hail of stones and ending in a bloody riot.

Years later, in 1910, another Englishman, Montague Brownslow Parker, paid hefty bribes to gain secret access to the southern part of the Temple Mount. A clandestine excavation ensued, in which Parker and his team used ropes lashed to the Shetiyyah, or "foundation stone" (floor of the Holy of Holies), to lower themselves into the Well of Souls. Yet once again the racket alerted a mosque attendant, who, inspecting the ruckus, recoiled to see foreigners hacking at holy ground with picks and shovels. He sounded the alarm, bringing enraged Muslim vigilantes racing to the scene. The explorers fled Jerusalem with an angry mob at their heels.[9]

The next reported attempt took place nearly a half century later, in the days immediately following the Six-Day War. Israeli forces ejected Jordanian troops from Jerusalem to regain control of the Temple Mount for the first time in almost two thousand years. For one brief month (June 1–July 7), the chaplain of the Israel Defense Forces, Rabbi Shlomo Goren, enjoyed complete jurisdiction over the site, though, regrettably, he didn't know what to do with it. His team of engineers spent two weeks surveying and mapping the Mount, but the mostly military detail had no clue how, or why, they should access the subterranean structures beneath. "I put them (engineers) inside the Temple Mount the first day after the liberation," he said, "but I didn't know what to look for! We could enter the Dome of the Rock to investigate beneath the rock itself; we could go everywhere, but we didn't."[10]

A month later, thinking to appease the Arab League and stave off a bloody *jihad* (holy war), Defense Minister Moshe Dayan returned the Mount to Islamic authority. His decision infuriated religious Jews, who already had initiated plans to tear down Islamic structures on Judaism's most holy site and start the process of building the third temple. An unprecedented opportunity clearly had been squandered, and fifteen years passed before another opportunity arose.

In July 1981, Rabbi Meir Yehuda Getz began construction on a new synagogue behind the Western Wall, facing the Temple Mount, when he accidentally broke into an underground catacomb known as the Warren's Gate cavern. This large, vaulted room, dating from the first temple period, once had been used for bringing in wood and materials for sacrifices and other temple rites. More importantly, according to Jewish tradition, Warren's Gate stood west of the temple and opened almost directly in front of the Holy of Holies.

Suspecting he'd stumbled upon a direct access to the deep caverns that once served as a cistern to the Mount, Getz mustered a ten-man excavation team and began clearing the great hall. For the next year and a half, his team worked feverishly in secret, wary of Muslim backlash and going to great lengths to avoid detection. The work progressed rapidly until, days before the team sensed it might penetrate the Holy of Holies, the local media broke the story. Outraged Islamic "Wakf" authorities dispatched a mob to attack the excavators; the Muslim Council called a general strike to halt the search, and the passage was quickly sealed.[11] To this day the vaults beneath the Temple Mount remain off-limits, as Israel and the PLO engage in a vicious fight over Palestinian statehood and sovereignty over these holy sites. The Mount itself continues its legacy as perhaps the world's preeminent archaeological riddle.

OTHER SITES, OTHER SEARCHES

Faced with such a state of affairs, it's not surprising that archaeologists, explorers, and fortune hunters have bundled up their picks and shovels and taken their excavations elsewhere. One such expedition involved an American named Larry Blaser, who searched the caves of Ein-Gedi, where, Jewish tradition tells us, David once hid from Saul. Another American, Vendyl Jones, dug among the caves of Wadi Jafet Zaben, north of Qumran, and unearthed a stash of reddish material thought to be a special incense used in temple worship. Neither excavation yielded evidence of the ark.

In the 1920s, American Antonia Frederick Futterer looked for the ark on Mount Nebo, where the Book of Maccabees suggests Jeremiah buried the sacred relic just prior to the Babylonian invasion. During his survey Futterer claims to have found a secret passage blocked by a wall etched with an ancient hieroglyph, which a Hebrew translator supposedly interpreted to read: "Herein Lies the Golden Ark of the Covenant." Curiously, Futterer never named the translator nor reproduced the inscription. And he never returned to the "secret passage" to retrieve the ark.[12]

Sixty years later another American explorer, Tom Crotser, borrowed the Futterer sketch to launch yet another search of

23

Mount Nebo, by now located just inside the border of the modern state of Jordan. Though he found nothing resembling Futterer's secret passage, his team moved on to neighboring Mount Pisgah, where Crotser said he found a gully blocked by a sheet of tin, concealing a narrow passage. From the gully the team hacked its way through a rock wall into an underground crypt, containing, insisted Crotser, a gold-covered, rectangular chest with carrying poles matching the biblical description of the ark. Predictably his color photographs of the object remained off-limits to all but a select circle of friends, who curiously refused to comment on the images. One who did, the respected archaeologist Siegfried H. Horn, rudely dismissed Futterer's so-called "ark" as nothing more than a modern, machine-fabricated, brass-plated box that had no relation to the ancient artifact.[13]

At least one modern-day inquiry placed its bets on the caves of the Mount of Olives, located directly across from the Temple Mount. While it's true that the Mount of Olives features many caves dating from the first temple era, the mountain, on both sides of the Kidron Valley, is riddled with Jewish, Christian and Muslim crypts. Owing primarily to Jewish laws of purity, it remains highly doubtful that Israel's holiest object would have been buried in the midst of a future cemetery.[14]

And then there are claims by amateur archaeologist Ron Wyatt, author of *Discovered—Noah's Ark*, of finding the ark of the covenant under the escarpment of Mount Calvary. Wyatt suggests that when Jesus died on the cross, his blood ran through the socket hole on Mount Calvary, dripped through a crack in the mountain, and finally landed on the mercy seat of the ark, located in a cavern below. In so doing, he said, Jesus' death consummated, in the most literal and exalted terms, the final blood atonement of God's ultimate High Priest—Jesus Christ! Wyatt says he broke through a layer of rock in a cave to reach the ark in a secret chamber. But when his Polaroid snap-shots of the object didn't turn out, he said he had to return at a later date with a borrowed "colonoscope" to drill a hole through the stone case surrounding the ark. This time, he claimed, he probed the case to conclude he had, indeed, found the sacred object.[15] Here I must say that my good friend, Bob Stuplich, accompanied Wyatt to this site and saw nothing.

So while many searchers have released numerous books and videos of their "discoveries," suffice it to say there is no hard evidence to suggest that the ark still resides in Jerusalem, under the Temple Mount, in a cave on Mount Calvary, or anywhere else in modern-day Israel.

Not until I began evaluating some of the theories, then vis-iting the relevant sites, did I seriously begin to doubt that any of these excavations would ever produce the ark. Even so, the more I learned, the less feasible it seemed that, after centuries in which these ancient landmarks had been repeatedly looted, explored, and excavated, the ark hadn't been found by *some-one*. As in my searches for Mount Sinai and Noah's ark, a fresh look at the subject convinced me that the so-called experts had it wrong and that the ark of the covenant likely lay someplace few suspected.

I discovered that the bulk of the theories, in fact, had been based more on legend and myth than a clear and unbiased read-ing of the Bible. While I had hoped I might find unexamined clues by searching Scripture, it was while reading *The Sign and the Seal* that I found myself entertaining an altogether different scenario, one that proposed a bizarre set of propositions—the weirdest being that the ark had been either abducted or smug-gled out of Jerusalem in the years before the first temple burned and then taken to a foreign land.

In the same way I'd learned to trust my instincts in my years as a police investigator, this notion struck me as far more plau-sible than the other theories. Of all the ideas tossed about by scholars and archaeologists, it was a curious legend from the biblical land of Cush that caught my attention, then caused my heart to swell. From among an endless collection of legends and theories, I found my gaze slowly turning to North Africa, to a country whose national identity seemed intertwined with the holy ark.

THREE

THE SIGN

Sometime after I returned from Robert Van Kampen's estate in the frigid winter of 1993, I read *The Sign and the Seal*, Graham Hancock's book about the ark of the covenant. While Hancock never claimed to be a Bible scholar, he was a noted journalist and tenacious investigator. His book presented a theory so outside traditional paradigms, however, that it sent shock waves through the staid archaeological community.

Hancock's six-hundred-page volume chronicles the ark of the covenant's presence in Ethiopia from ancient history to the present day. Its occasionally numbing detail made the book difficult to plow through, yet the author's investigative journalism skills pulled me along.

Could the ark of the covenant actually exist today? I doubted such a proposal, yet as I waded through *The Sign and the Seal*, my mind yielded to the amazing ideas he proposed. A body of historical evidence emerged from Hancock's years of relentless journalistic research which seemed to cut through layers of murky traditions. Little did I know it then, but my foray into this fascinating subject would result in my own discoveries—discoveries that would ultimately present new possibilities for biblical prophecy and scriptural interpretation.

WHEN DID THE ARK DISAPPEAR?

From Hancock's book, I discovered that no one knew for sure when the ark of the covenant disappeared from Solomon's temple. This had to be the most incredible mystery of all time—right down my alley.

As an ex-police investigator, I love solving a real whodunit. The quintessential question surrounding the ark of the covenant is, *who did it?* Which ancient king of Israel allowed the ark of the covenant to go missing on his watch? Someone, somewhere in time, allowed the most holy object in all of recorded history to vanish—a blunder of incalculable magnitude.

Part of the quandary surrounding the disappearance of the ark can be explained by the divinely ordained practice of allowing only one person each year, on one day—the Day of Atonement—to even *see* the ark. On that most holy day the high priest would enter the Holy of Holies carrying animal blood for atonement, a sacrifice for the sins of the people. He would sprinkle the blood on the ark and in front of the ark and thus fulfill God's specific instructions.

Through Hancock's research I came to understand that the person most likely responsible for allowing the ark of the covenant to be taken from Solomon's Temple was a king by the name of Manasseh, one of the most evil rulers of all time. The Bible claims that Manasseh . . .

> did evil in the sight of the LORD, according to the abominations of the nations whom the LORD had cast out before the children of Israel. For he rebuilt the high

places which Hezekiah his father had destroyed; he raised up altars for Baal, and made a wooden image, as Ahab king of Israel had done; and he worshiped all the host of heaven and served them. He also built altars in the house of the LORD, of which the LORD had said, "In Jerusalem I will put My name." And he built altars for all the host of heaven in the two courts of the house of the LORD. Also he made his son pass through the fire, practiced soothsaying, used witchcraft, and consulted spiritists and mediums. He did much evil in the sight of the LORD, to provoke *Him* to anger. He even set a carved image of Asherah that he had made, in the house of which the LORD had said to David and to Solomon his son, "In this house and in Jerusalem, which I have chosen out of all the tribes of Israel, I will put My name forever. . . ." Moreover Manasseh shed very much innocent blood, till he had filled Jerusalem from one end to another, besides his sin by which he made Judah sin, in doing evil in the sight of the LORD (2 Kings 21:2–7, 16 NKJV italics added).

Scripture describes a maniacal, evil, despicable person, a vile man who so mocked God, defiled his holy temple, and performed such unspeakable acts that the Levitical priests would have been repulsed by his rule. I knew that the ark of the covenant would not have been allowed to remain in the Holy of Holies while idols were placed in the temple; the priests simply would not have allowed it.

Just a few generations earlier, eighty angry priests physically threw King Uzziah out of the temple when he attempted to offer his own incense; then God struck him with leprosy (2 Chron. 26:16–21). If this happened to King Uzziah for unlawfully offering incense, then how much more scandalized would the priests have felt when King Manasseh attempted to

29

∧

move idols into the Holy of Holies, the resting place of the ark of the covenant?

As a result of Manasseh's unfathomable irreverence, God pronounced a grave sentence on Israel: "Behold, I am bringing such calamity upon Jerusalem and Judah, that whoever hears of it, both his ears will tingle. And I will stretch over Jerusalem the measuring line of Samaria and the plummet of the house of Ahab; I will wipe Jerusalem as one wipes a dish, wiping it and turning it upside down" (2 Kings 21:12–13 NKJV).

But how could we know for sure that Manasseh allowed the ark to be taken away during his reign? I already knew that the Bible strongly indicates that the ark still remained in the temple during the reign of Manasseh's father, King Hezekiah. When threatened by the Assyrian king, Hezekiah prayed to God "who dwells between the cherubim" (2 Kings 19:15 NKJV)—a phrase referring to the golden angels that were part of the mercy seat atop the ark of the covenant. This means that the ark most assuredly remained in Solomon's Temple during the time of Hezekiah, just prior to Manasseh.

I also knew that during the reign of Josiah, two kings after Manasseh, the ark was no longer in the temple, since Josiah told the priests to "put the holy ark in the house which Solomon the son of David, king of Israel, built. It shall no longer be a burden on your shoulders. Now serve the LORD your God and His people Israel" (2 Chron. 35:3 NKJV). The verb "put" in this verse indicates that the ark was not in the temple, while the phrase, "it shall no longer be a burden on your shoulders," indicates that the ark was being carried in correct Levitical fashion (Num. 7:9), perhaps to some location outside Jerusalem. The Levites carried the ark on their shoulders only when transporting it from one location to another. These clues seem to indicate:

1. The ark remained in the temple during the reign of Hezekiah, who prayed to God "who dwells between the cherubim."
2. The ark was absent from the temple during the reign of Josiah (the Levites carried it on their shoulders to an unknown location).
3. Therefore, the ark most likely disappeared during the reign of Manasseh (or possibly during the rule of Amon, Manasseh's son, who ruled for two years before being assassinated).

31

Λ

Once Hancock felt satisfied that he had assembled a likely historical sequence behind the ark's disappearance, there remained yet another question: where did it go?

Hancock turned to the Falasha Jews from Ethiopia. He flew to Israel to interview Falasha elders airlifted to Jerusalem during Operation Moses in 1984. In Jerusalem Hancock found a patriarch named Raphael Hadane.

Hadane said that traditions handed down by his ancestors indicated that before migrating to Ethiopia, they had first lived in Egypt's southern Nile region, in the area of today's Aswan. Hancock discovered that a colony of Hebrews had indeed settled in that region, on Elephantine Island in the Nile, during the reign of wicked King Manasseh. Papyrus scrolls found by archaeologists on Elephantine Island indicate that a substantial Hebrew settlement existed there between the seventh and fifth centuries B.C. Even more significant, the refugees constructed a temple whose dimensions and appearance—exterior pillars, gateways of stone, roof of cedarwood—had been modeled precisely on Solomon's Temple. Papyrus records also recorded that the Hebrews performed ritual animal sacrifices at the Elephantine temple, just as in Jerusalem, including the all-important sacrifice of a lamb during Passover. Other papyri spoke of God literally "dwelling there."[1] From Hancock's perspective (as from mine), the Elephantine Hebrews clearly believed Yahweh resided literally in their temple.

Incredibly, the Elephantine temple of Yahweh was destroyed in 410 B.C., within sixty years of the date legends say the ark arrived in Ethiopia (470 B.C.). Ethiopian tradition says that from Elephantine Island the ark migrated south to a huge lake called Lake Tana in the highlands of Ethiopia, where it lay hidden for nearly eight hundred years on the remote island of Tana Kirkos. Even today the island is still considered a holy place.

Hancock's research created a historical scenario that seemed both reasonable and logical, even though it conflicted with a cultural myth prominent throughout Ethiopia. That myth tells how the ark was brought to Ethiopia by Menelik, the illegitimate son of Solomon and the Queen of Sheba, shortly after the time of Solomon. As provocative and widespread as is this Ethiopian tradition, careful research reveals that the ark remained in the temple long after Solomon's day. The legend of Menelik has no basis in fact or history.

Hancock concluded that the ark had indeed reached Ethiopia, traveling by way of Elephantine Island and then on to Tana Kirkos Island.

THE ETHIOPIAN CONNECTION

Following this historical "trail of crumbs," Hancock traveled to Lake Tana, chartered a boat, and docked at Tana Kirkos Island.

Tana Kirkos—its high cliffs and dense jungle rising up out of the lake like a haunted castle—boasts a number of ancient artifacts, altars, and stone pillars. All seem to spring from the pages of the Old Testament, whispering of an ancient Hebrew culture. The monks showed Hancock a slab of stone high on a ledge where, they said, blood sacrifices had once been performed next to a portable tabernacle (tent), under which the ark had apparently sat for eight hundred years. The chief monk explained that in A.D. 330, when Ethiopia converted to Christianity, King Ezana's troops took the ark from the Jewish priests on Tana Kirkos and installed it in a great church in Axum, where he said it remains today.

I knew from my police background that if Hancock had stumbled upon only one or two puzzle pieces, his findings could easily be dismissed. I could then be forgiven for setting his book aside and forgetting about the whole thing.

Yet while Hancock had searched for every reason to abandon the project, he continued to stumble upon clue after clue leading him back to Ethiopia. He had tried repeatedly to disqualify Axum as a viable candidate but couldn't, and today there are no viable alternatives and no proofs that the relic has been destroyed.

Hancock failed in his final attempt in January 1991 to see the Axum ark; he never managed to get any closer than the fence encircling the sanctuary chapel. Yet this setback didn't diminish his theory. He had conducted a rigorous investigation, and for that he deserves all the credit.

Still many questions lingered. No westerner had actually ever *seen* the ark. What did Axum's relic look like? And why Ethiopia? Why Axum? What role would this region play if the ark ever appeared once more on the world stage?

I knew myself well enough to know that I would always wonder unless I personally tested these theories. Since the day I gazed upon Hollywood's ark of the covenant in the blockbuster film *Raiders of the Lost Ark,* the quest to find the ark struck me as the most thrilling of all adventures.

After much thought and prayer, I decided to take up the gauntlet and look into the matter firsthand. Though I didn't know what I'd find or where I would go, I set about planning my first trip to Ethiopia, stepping eagerly, and blindly, into what would become the biggest adventure of my life.

FOUR

EYE ON AXUM

My good friend, Joby Book—born in
Louisiana, reared in Houston, and living in
Arkansas—could best be described as a "good
ol' boy." Besides his slow, southern drawl, he
somehow manages to insert the expression,
"Hey, Bubba!" into every third sentence.

I enjoy Joby's company, and on one trip
down south in the winter of 1997, I told him
the story of the ark in Ethiopia. Excited, he
asked me if he might tag along, should I ever
visit Africa. To my surprise, he told his physi-
cian wife, Lindy, about our conversation, and
she promptly contributed the funds I needed
for the trip—with the condition that I take
along her husband. "He needs to get away,"
she whispered as she handed me the check.
"He needs an adventure."

How could I refuse?

That first trip fell into place with relative
ease. Lindy's donation arrived in the middle of
winter, when my schedule typically experienced a lull. With funds in hand, I immediately
began booking flights and planning a whirl-
wind itinerary. Suddenly, after four years of
plotting and dreaming, I found myself with

both the time and the resources to indulge my growing fascination with the ark. I called my friend, helicopter pilot Chuck Aaron, who'd spent a rushed afternoon in Axum earlier that summer, and asked him what I should pack and where I should stay.

"I don't know on either count," he said. "It was pretty hot there when I visited, but Axum's at a pretty high altitude. I don't know what winter's like. A crew was in the process of building a hotel when I passed through, but I don't know if it's finished."

"What if it's not?" I asked.

"Kill yourself," he replied—a joke, I hoped. "Axum's a horrible place to be without a hotel."

With those uplifting words, I had my travel agent book two round-trip international flights from New York City to Rome, then south to Addis Ababa.

ADDIS ABABA

Descending into Addis Ababa in the first rays of dawn, one can gaze down through the clouds and see the lazy, sun-washed southern Nile Valley where it vanishes into Sudan's vast eastern desert.

Stretching like a great sand ocean into Ethiopia's northern Entoto mountains, the blistering wilderness softens into a rolling, blonde-baked sea of foothills surrounding Addis. Odd-shaped mounds and outcroppings are crowned with flat-topped trees and bushy eucalyptus imported from Australia. Palm-thatched huts on every other hilltop lend the landscape an otherworldly appearance, recalling the strangely sculpted sandstone contours and bluffs of northern New Mexico. Even prior to landing, this airborne view provided me a glimpse of the rugged Horn of Africa, gateway to the Dark Continent, a land springing forth, it seemed, from a Salvador Dali still life.

Located at the heart of Ethiopia and saddled with a population approaching five million, Addis Ababa is a teeming Third World metropolis, awash in poverty while balancing the lifestyles and customs of a multitude of ethnic groups and cultures. Addis grew out of a small military encampment used by Emperor Menelik II in 1886 and by the turn of the century had grown into Ethiopia's largest city. Crisscrossed today by many modern roads, railways, and bridges, it seems to be making strides—through its modest offerings of museums, universities, and cuisine—toward becoming the cosmopolitan center its tourist brochures describe. And, indeed, boasting more than seventy embassies and consular representatives, Addis today stands as the unchallenged diplomatic capital of Africa.

Driving in from the airport, our taxi passed through many wooded hillsides and gullies cut with fast-flowing streams. I noted a variety of small but colorful commercial districts—cozy espresso bars, fruit stands, jewelry, antique and clothing boutiques—nestled among an occasional palace or government skyscraper. Yet vast parts of the city sit isolated from these tiny pinpoints of prosperity.

The handful of luxury hotels, built on fortress hilltops bedecked with fragrant gardens of bougainvillea, can't disguise the city's squalid underside. These castles of new commerce stare out over fetid slums and often sit side by side with filthy ghettos crawling with crippled beggars and panhandling children. Addis clearly aspires to be more than it is, yet it remains a place where prostitution and AIDS run rampant among an aimless youth, where skilled workers earn about two dollars a day, and where swarms of sickly children have neither enough to eat nor rudimentary medical care. In every respect, Addis Ababa is a metaphor for Africa itself.

Our short layover allowed Joby and me to tour some of the city's wide, tree-lined streets and bustling outdoor markets. There I observed the common Third World incongruity of tall, modern office buildings, elegant villas, and marble conference halls surrounded by shabby, wattle and daub shanties, and smooth boulevards bordered by cart paths overrun with scrawny cattle, sheep, goats, and chickens.

Everywhere we went, locals in white, homespun cotton robes and dresses strolled arm-in-arm to the markets or churches. It became immediately clear that church and religious ceremonies remain a major feature of Ethiopian life. The Ethiopian Orthodox Church burst to prominence in the fourth century, far earlier than in Europe, and today enjoys a nearly autonomous stature within the country. I found its lavish pageantry and colorful iconography reminiscent of Western Catholicism; Ethiopians celebrate some 150 saints days a year and hold Mary, mother of Christ, in highest regard. I also found it interesting that in many of the city's parks and plazas stand towering stone and metal sculptures of lions—including one enormous lion of Judah dominating a square near the center of the city—exalting Ethiopia's Hebrew roots with an openness and grandeur I hadn't expected.

It made me recall that until the Mengistu regime's violent "reforms," the Ethiopian national flag had prominently incorporated the lion of Judah in its tricolor design. In its official artwork, the country appears almost to perceive itself as a lost tribe of Israel. I could hardly wait to behold the jewel in the empire's crown, the spiritual heart and soul of Ethiopia: Axum.

INTO AXUM

Next morning Joby and I rose early to catch a small, twin-prop Fokker 50 to Axum. We flew north across a brown, deeply furrowed countryside, into endless miles of gritty hills and desolate canyons—a wild, inhospitable land interrupted only at great intervals by puny stands of green stubble sprigging up like brush bristles.

Further north the countryside became a Gobi Desert-like prairie of red clay, painted bluffs, and angling arroyos—a chalk-dry wasteland interspersed with dust-caked patches of green that I took to be primitive agricultural fieldwork. Here and there on cream-colored hilltops, I saw the coarse mills of dirt farmers threshing *teff*—a wheatlike grain that Ethiopians grind, ferment, and bake to make sour-tasting *injera*, the national dish. Enjoying the diverse panorama from above, I recalled how Axum, until the early 1990s, had been locked in a bloody guerilla war, squeezed between rebel forces and Mengistu's long-range cannons. The conflict decimated the countryside for miles, and many graves still pepper these craggy hills.

As we neared Axum, our pilot suddenly cut the engines and began a steep, banking descent. Swooping out of the sky at a nearly vertical pitch, our plane leveled out just in time to send scores of shepherds and their flocks scurrying for cover. As we arced back skyward, I looked down to see that this badly rutted, washed-out pasture—where men in filthy white robes used sticks to shoo grazing cows and camels out of the way—would serve as our landing strip. Craning my neck as we circled around, I held my breath as the pilot took a second pass at the runway, hitting the ground with a crunch and sending rocks and debris slamming into the bottom of the wings and denting the plane's undercarriage. The plane shuddered down a washboard runway that would have loosened the lug nuts on a Humvee, braking to a stop in a swirl of dust a few yards from a barbed-wire fence.

I turned to see Joby's white face and realized that my own neck and forehead poured sweat. In all of my travels and of all the risks I've taken during countless dangerous escapades, I've grown to loathe these whiplashing, semi-crash landings at backwater airfields. For me, the thought of touching down on such primitive surfaces seemed nearly suicidal. Yet these gutsy Ethiopian Airlines pilots do it every day.

Joby and I gathered ourselves and our bags and stepped out into the blinding sunshine. A dry breeze blew my face dry. Along with a few Axumites lugging bulky canvas bundles on their shoulders, we clambered down the steps to behold the most primitive, ramshackle airport I'd ever encountered. Strewn about the periphery sat several burned-out, bullet-riddled shells of military planes, military trucks, and assorted chunks of battlefield refuse. Mangy sheep nibbled at grass growing up through shrapnel holes in the rusted metal carcasses.

We'd been told the airport was a bit crude, but this pathetic depot defied my worst expectations. It consisted of little more than a knobby frame of wooden poles lashed together by wire. Sheets of corrugated tin had been nailed up to form crude walls and a roof, and beams of sunlight bled through yawning gaps in the ill-fitting panels. A little hand-painted sign hung on a rusty nail, telling us we'd reached the "Axum Terminal"—a leaky structure no more than thirty feet by twenty feet.

As we crossed the pasture to retrieve our luggage, we passed an old, bearded man in a ratty robe sitting on a stool by the front door. "Look at *that*," Joby said in his Southern drawl. He pointed to a spot behind the old man. There, quivering in the shadows, swarmed thousands of bees, flowing in and out of a large hive perched high on a wall inside the terminal. The drone of rushing wings unsettled the otherwise quiet noontime air. I recoiled to see bees crawling all over the man, head to foot, covering his ears, neck, and beard. *What kind of macabre circus is this?* I wondered. Amazingly, the old fellow paid the bees no mind, seeming unconcerned with the buzzing necklace.

"That is unbelievable," Joby said. I nodded, turning my gaze to adjacent fields that had been pressed into service as an airport, still grazed by sheep and assorted African barnyard critters. We heard the roar of an engine and turned to see our plane clattering across the pasture, lifting off and finally disappearing over a steep sweep of red-brown cliffs. The gust knocked Joby's hat off, sending it cartwheeling down the rutted dirt path.

That's when the first wave of flies hit—thick clouds of buzzing, stinging flies, aiming for our mouths, eyes, and noses. From that moment on they waged a relentless assault. Piles of animal dung lay everywhere, and I quickly recalled that we had landed in a part of Ethiopia that had endured endless cycles of famine and disease.

The feeling of isolation we felt at that moment unnerved both of us. We stood silently for several minutes, listening as our plane's engines faded into the southern horizon. Joby finally broke the silence: "Welcome to the end of the world."

For Joby it appeared to be the end of the world, but after a few moments I began to feel right at home. I rather enjoyed the stark surroundings. The flies, the bees, and the dilapidated terminal transported us into the rugged heart of exotic, mysterious Africa.

Soon a young man in his early twenties strode up. "Hello," he said in clear English. "I am Ecuba. I would be honored to serve as your guide."

Ecuba seemed to appear from thin air. He had a big, toothy grin and smiling, round face; he wore a T-shirt, sandals, and faded Levis. "If you come with me," he continued, "I will take you to get food and water."

I looked him over, then scanned our present surroundings. "Ecuba, huh?" He seemed nice enough, and we certainly didn't know anybody else in Axum. "All right. Is there a hotel in town?"

"Yes," he said with a nod, "there is a hotel that will accommodate you."

"How much?" I asked, but Joby jerked my arm.

"I don't care *what* it costs," he whispered through clenched teeth. "Pay him the money, and let's get *out* of this fly trap."

Before I could relay his sentiment, Joby put his hand on Ecuba's shoulder and squeezed firmly. "Just take us to the hotel," he said and reached for his wallet. "We'll pay whatever you ask!"

FiVE

CITY OF PRAYER

The van ride from the airport took us through the heart of Axum, into the marketplace, and past the most bizarre pageant of humanity I'd ever witnessed.

The dusty road, lined with slow-advancing ranks of men, women, and children, teemed with wobbly caravans of miniature donkeys, camels, and cows burdened with huge bundles. Pint-sized burros strained under bales of sticks nearly twice their size. Camels carted mounds of rugs and other hand-spun textiles. Bearded men in long robes and thin sandals shuffled by, groaning under sheaves of cowhides balanced delicately on their heads. Women in ankle-length, dirt-smudged dresses hauled twenty-gallon water jugs lashed to their backs with ropes. And even small children, many with crosses gouged into their foreheads, dragged bulky water jugs on flimsy, wooden wagons.

Ecuba explained that a lengthy drought had prompted water rationing, requiring the locals to manually cart water over great distances. This daily, even hourly labor put men, women, and children on the same footing as animals, all of them toiling as sweaty beasts of burden in the heat of the day.

En route I explained to Ecuba why we'd come. He replied that he knew chapel monks in town who might be willing to answer our questions. I felt a pang of nerves, wondering how well I'd interface with the devout order on their sacred turf.

We entered the city and saw on a hillside Axum's renowned stone obelisks peeking through the trees like Africa's version of Stonehenge. Quarried from single pieces of granite, these thousand-year-old columns (shaped like mini-Washington Monuments) are believed to be either royal burial stones or victory markers commemorating great military conquests. To this day no one knows how they were made, transported, or erected. The sight of them reminded me that we'd come to a place where truth and fiction coexist.

As I'd expected, the city exuded a mysterious, Old Testament feel. The tan, brush-covered slopes and scattered ruins looked as old and sunbaked as time itself. Like scattered shards of broken pottery, the knobby hills whispered of vanquished kings and fallen kingdoms, of secrets long concealed. Among these scruffy ravines and hidden canyons, the history of Ethiopia and that of the ark of the covenant had become inseparably linked. As we rumbled along in our rickety cab, Ecuba pointed out a battery of red rock ruins to our right.

"These are the remains of Sheba's palace," he said.

We stopped to take a quick look around. Surprised at the size and advanced architecture of the ruins—including an intricate, multiterraced flagstone floor, supposedly Sheba's private bathing area, extensive kitchens and brick ovens, and a well-appointed throne room—I wondered that structures so old could be so well preserved.

"Are you tellin' me that the queen of Sheba actually lived *here?*" Joby asked as we climbed a narrow flight of steps to a broad, sun-washed landing.

"Not according to most scholars," I shrugged. "The dates don't line up."

But as I stood in the arid breeze, gazing back toward Axum's leaning obelisks, I didn't really care whether or not this sprawling palace once housed Sheba's court. I hadn't been in town an hour, and already I could see why the city had come to be regarded in northern Africa as the Second Jerusalem.[1]

For those few minutes I allowed myself to forget that when the biblical queen of Sheba traveled to Jerusalem to meet King Solomon in approximately 900 B.C., Axum likely didn't exist—at least, not as the important religious and cultural center it would become several hundred years later. Archaeology suggests that Solomon reigned almost a thousand years before any settlers came to Axum, around the beginning of the first century A.D.[2]

"By this timetable," I told Joby, "no serious scholar would suggest the Axumite kingdom grew to a stature befitting Sheba much before the birth of Christ."

Of course, by then, Axum had grown into the capital of a far-reaching kingdom of culture and commerce, dominating for a millennium the vital crossroads of Africa and Asia. The first reports of this highly developed civilization come from A.D. 64, when Greek author Periplus described Axum's ruler as "a prince superior to most and educated with a knowledge of Greek."[3] Centuries later a Roman ambassador named Julian glowingly described Axum as "the greatest city of all Ethiopia," whose king wore garments of linen embroidered with gold from his waist to his loins and rode about on a towering, four-wheeled chariot shingled with gold plates and drawn by elephants.[4]

These images of splendor describe one of the most powerful capitals between the Roman Empire and Persia—a power that sent merchant navies sailing as far away as Egypt, India, Ceylon, and China. It boasted a sophisticated culture that adopted Christianity as its state religion as early as the fourth century A.D.

Not so in Solomon's time. At the height of his reign, some twelve hundred years prior, the region of Abyssinia could best be described as a land of savages.

As expected, little of Axum's regal past emerged for Joby and me. Today the town is hot and dirty, its people hungry and impoverished. Ecuba drove us to the market square, where row after dreary row of dust-caked tarpaulins hung slack above hundreds of emaciated peasant merchants. These vacant-eyed unfortunates sat squatting, knees to chin, next to puny piles of produce and knickknacks.

One toothless vendor tried to sell us a shriveled gourd. Another held out two scrawny chickens, tied by their feet, while another brandished three meager scoops of ground cumin on a snatch of rag. I found it nearly overwhelming, navigating row after row of filthy stalls filled with hundreds of dirt-poor villagers. Everyone sat hunkered and somber in the scorching sun, selling the same things—a couple of dirty eggs, a few shriveled limes, a piece of raw, fly-infested meat, a clove or two of garlic—hoping, praying, to sell *something* for a few pennies.

The overpowering odor of goat and cow dung filled the air, burning our nostrils and drawing endless clouds of flies. Most of the children we saw had bloated tummies and rags for clothes. Worst of all, I saw that the flies swarmed upon the smallest children, who stood crying while black, buzzing clumps fixed themselves to their noses, eyes, and mouths. Throughout Africa these flies lay eggs in children's eyes, producing the red, festering eye slits that too often presage childhood blindness. Most of these afflictions could be cured by a quick round of antibiotics and a dose or two of antiseptic eye cream, yet even crude medical care remains unavailable to these people. Everywhere we went, begging men without legs scuffled about on blocks of wood while children with ankles hugely swollen held out desperate hands, whispering, "Mister, Mister," hoping for a coin.

Oh Axum, I thought, *how far you have fallen!*

THE ARK CULT

The Yeha Hotel sits high on a hill overlooking the city. By American standards, it is an inconvenient affair, with frequent water and electric outages. For us, however, it was a welcome surprise.

From its broad terrace visitors can gaze down at Axum's stone obelisks, nudged against a west-facing hillside. Across a courtyard sets a massive Byzantine dome. Beyond that lay the fifteenth-century roofs and turrets of the famous cathedrals of St. Mary of Zion. With a stream of white-robed worshipers marching silently back and forth, Axum below appeared to be a lazy, tree-shaded retreat overrun with religious pilgrims.

After lunch Ecuba left us briefly, and Joby and I took rooms, organized our gear, and ate lunch, a tasty variation of spaghetti and red sauce. The fascist Italian occupation of the 1930s indoctrinated Ethiopia into the joys of Italian cooking, and even the most obscure restaurants feature fairly passable pasta dishes at the top of their menus. Ecuba returned shortly, holding an old man by the hand.

"This is Birani Miscal," he said, "which means, 'light of the cross.' I believe he will be able to answer your questions."

Just then Joby returned, refreshed and composed from his room. "Who's that?" he whispered.

"Ecuba's friend," I replied with a shrug, sizing up the old fellow. He looked ancient, his black face brazed and puckered by the sun. A smattering of yellow teeth interrupted massive gaps in his smile. "It is my pleasure to meet you," I said, extending a hand.

Birani greeted us in return, holding his left hand over his mouth as he spoke. At first I thought he meant to hide his teeth, but Ecuba explained: "It is a habit he formed through decades of translating the old manuscripts. They must bend over ancient scrolls in the church vaults."

I turned to Birani, who bowed lightly and clarified: "It prevents moisture from my mouth from contaminating the manuscripts," he said with a thick, raspy accent—Tigrigna being the local language—then removed his hand long enough to reveal a feisty smile and deep laugh lines around his eyes.

Ecuba left us with Birani, who escorted Joby and me down the hill, across a field, and into Axum's expansive church compound. There we entered a shaded, mud-walled courtyard surrounding an old stucco church. Judging by the wails blaring over the speakers, prayer services had begun.

Hardly bigger than a one-room schoolhouse, the church had been an Axum landmark for three hundred years. Its heavy, wood-grain doors were now stained and sandblasted black by wind and sun. Birani whispered that, fifty yards to the west, through the trees and stucco fortifications, "sits the chapel that houses the ark." To this point neither Joby nor I had mentioned the ark. His unsolicited remark encouraged me.

"Well, shoot," Joby blurted out, "let's go have a look."

We might both have bolted off across the field had not Birani held us back. He gestured toward the big, moss-covered rock wall that, by appearances, granted men access to the church and kept women out. Massed around the outside of the wall, nearly filling a field, knelt hundreds of women wrapped in linen, praying, chanting hymns, and uttering melodic devotions that sounded, to my untrained ear, slightly Jewish.

"What are all these women doing here?" I asked.

"They come here every day to pray," he said. "They are not allowed to go inside the church. It is a holy site. Many of them cannot bear children, so they pray to the ark of the covenant for a child."

Pray *to* the ark? For a child? *What's that about?* I wondered. *Do they consider God and the ark interchangeable?* I felt suddenly confused and wanted to say something. Instead I decided to listen.

"If a barren woman becomes pregnant, she devotes her firstborn son to the hermitage," Birani continued, pointing toward a cluster of old buildings nearby. "There the boys learn a life of devotion and spend their days reading Scripture and fasting." He paused, then added: "It is where they become initiated into the ways of the ark."

From this short exchange it seemed the ark—or what they believed to be the ark—occupied an exalted status. That came as no surprise, but if I understood Birani correctly, it appeared as if all of Axum revolved around a sort of ark cult, whereby young and old alike pray to the object as a deity unto itself. I watched the women praying next to the wall. Had the relic become to them a graven image? I knew these people to be Christians of a sort, in possession of what might be an ancient Hebrew artifact. That raised questions of its own—such as why *Christians* would incorporate a Jewish artifact into their non-Jewish religious ceremonies—but I hadn't expected this.

Surrounded by so much symbolic imagery, I grew suddenly impatient, yearning to pull Birani aside and ask him to arrange an interview with the guardian monk. I held back. Certain questions cannot be broached in these cultures until a measure of trust has developed.

As I watched the praying throng, however, I pondered the reality of their "miracle babies," consigned to a childhood of religious indoctrination, worship, and temple service. The hermitage system, it seemed, groomed the boys to become apprentice monks, schooled in the mysteries of the ark. They spent their youth in a cloistered compound, pledged to a life of celibacy and poverty. It faintly echoed of the life of Samuel, whose barren mother prayed for a son, then promptly delivered him to the tabernacle after his birth, where he grew into one of Israel's greatest prophets (1 Sam. 1:24).

Axum's hermitage seemed to be based on the same arrangement: grateful mothers repaying God's blessing with a sacrificial act. Eyeing the small boys in white robes marching lightly about the compound, running chores, attending to the older monks, I wondered how it all fit into Ethiopia's Orthodox Christian doctrine.

Certainly their faith incorporated distinctive Old Testament practices, such as Levitical food proscriptions and observance of the Sabbath. But did it also include praying to and living one's life in service of the ark? Did these African Christians worship Jesus, or had they lapsed through countless generations into a subtle ark idolatry? Did the hermitage boys grow into men who feared and exalted an object rather than a living Savior? I'd only just arrived and didn't have enough information to make such judgments, but my initial impressions set me on edge.

The women appeared to kneel and cry out to the ark for children. I almost asked Birani to enlighten me but realized that he, too, had grown up in the system and might receive my question defensively. There would be time later to discuss sensitive matters, some of which I suspected cut to the heart of Axumite Orthodoxy.

PRAYER STICKS AND POP SONGS

Joby and I trailed Birani into the small church where two hundred bearded, white-turbaned men stood rigidly in place, eyes closed, praying. Some propped their chins on tall sticks—"praying sticks," Birani explained, handing us two from a tall wooden chamber on the back wall.

Sensing our interest in Axum's spiritual community, Birani assumed we'd enjoy a good, old-fashioned Ethiopian prayer meeting. From our perch at the back of the church, things seemed to be heating up. Nobody looked up or paid the Americans in khaki safari gear any mind whatsoever. All had lapsed into a deep state of worship, chanting a sing-song elegy that, though recited in Tigrigna, soothed me by its reverberating cadence.

Propping my chin on a padded prayer stick, I started praying in my own language. After several minutes I found myself parroting our hosts' mesmerizing incantations. Three hours passed before I knew it. When I raised my head, nobody had moved from their spot. I couldn't tell if Joby had fallen asleep. His eyes remained closed, his whole being tilted awkwardly against his stick.

Standing in the shadows, I watched narrow beams of light trickling in from a wood-slat lattice high on a wall, illuminating a musty gallery of weathered paintings. Some depicted Jesus, the apostles, and Mary; others featured angelic hosts and local saints. The chapel's foot-thick walls and recessed cupolas had a smooth, burnished texture, as if centuries of smoke, incense, and human sweat had buffed every surface.

Finally there came a short recess in prayer, prompted by an oddly familiar sound, faintly audible. After a few seconds I recognized it as a song I once knew. I turned to see a plastic wall clock hanging by a piece of twine. I did a double take to see a cartoon photo of Tony Orlando and Dawn glaring down from its parakeet yellow cabinet. Its mini-speaker chimed a tinny version of "Tie a Yellow Ribbon Round the Old Oak Tree." How had this radio come to be hanging on the wall of one of the most sacred churches in Ethiopia? Joby opened his eyes and instantly burst out laughing. I gave him a sharp jab with my elbow. In these staid, solemn quarters, the monks missed the comic incongruity. To them the song served as an alarm, signaling a break in prayers; once it ended, they resumed their positions.

Joby shook beside me, trying to stifle his laughter. "Bob, that blows my mind!" he whispered. "That just blows my mind!"

Some of the monks turned to look. Birani cupped a hand to his ear and glanced Joby's way.

"What does he *say?*" Birani asked in thick Tigrigna.

I'd grown used to it. Joby's accent, stickier than tar, befuddled everyone in Africa, even Ethiopians who spoke perfect English. I had to translate for him wherever we went.

51
Λ

"My friend is surprised to hear an American song in your beautiful church," I said, pointing to the wall clock. Birani shrugged and led us back outside into the blinding sunlight.

I decided the time had come. "Birani," I said, "would you consider introducing me to the guardian of the ark?"

Birani slapped a hand over his mouth and shook his head politely but firmly. "No, it is impossible to see the guardian," he said. "I cannot do this. Not now."

Without elaborating, he walked briskly across the church grounds, beckoning us to follow. He led us to the St. Mary of Zion chapel complex—a spacious, walled compound dominated on opposite ends by two old and austere-looking churches. I knew that somewhere within this historic maze sat the sepulcher of the ark; for here, as elsewhere, crowds of men, women, and children stood, sat, or knelt in various stages of genuflection. The oldest men sat under scrawny trees, wrapped up in heavy, multicolored prayer shawls and blankets, a pot of water by their side. Others leaned against medieval-era, rock-and-mortar pillars, reading red-bound Bibles. The entire plaza seemed awash in ghostly shadows—a citywide congregation lost in a trance of personal devotion, noses buried in Ge'ez translations of the Scriptures, mouthing silent prayers.

CHURCHES AND CHAPELS

As we strolled these ancient footpaths into the center of Ethiopia's religious ancestry, we noticed pilgrims occasionally casting a furtive glance our way. I'd never seen anything like it—an entire community lost for hours in prayer, worshiping spellbound amid a network of churches and chapels dating to the birth of African Christianity.

The first church we passed, the now famous St. Mary of Zion Church—half castle, half church—loomed large and statuesque. It had been erected in the mid-seventeenth century by Emperor Fasilidas, who, in anointing Axum the empire's spiritual heartland, distinguished St. Mary of Zion Church as one of Ethiopia's most revered Christian shrines. Its timeworn, stonework facade sported medieval turrets and arched windows with multicolored lattice slats, crowned by notched battlements, as if straight from Camelot.

"The church is the intellectual capital of the Axumite state," Birani said proudly; and, indeed, from this four-hundred-year-old citadel, the Amharic-Christian culture spiraled outward and planted spiritual roots that anchor Ethiopian Orthodoxy today.[5]

Across the complex stood the much newer St. Mary of Zion Cathedral, eye-catching among the rustic monuments for its massive, paneled dome and Persian-influenced fixtures. The basilica came into being in the 1960s at Emperor Haile Selassie's bidding, and Britain's Queen Elizabeth II thought enough of the occasion to attend its dedication. To me, its globe-shaped spire, gilded arrows, and astrological symbols looked more like the crown of a wizard's scepter, or perhaps a Turkish mosque, than a Christian prayer center. A tall bell tower stood beside it, tapered at the top and obviously styled after the town's famous stelae.

We kept walking. Between the two churches sat a deep, mossy trough, grown over with grass and filled in with chunks of rubble and ancient stone abutments. This trench, Birani told us, contained the ruins of the original Saint Mary of Zion Church, built in the fourth century A.D. by King Ezana as a memorial to Ethiopia's dramatic conversion to Christianity.

"It is the most sacred place in all Ethiopia," he said, staring into the pit. I knew from my own research that we stared into the bowels of the earliest Christian church on the African continent.[6] Though one can barely make it out today, its foundation stones had once been part of an extensive church (and, likely, the first chapel in Axum to house the ark). Unfortunately, it had been razed by Ahmed Gragn, a fanatical Muslim invader.

A visiting Portuguese priest named Francisco Alvares depicted the church in 1526 as a "five-aisled basilica with seven oriented altars"; it reportedly had sheltered the ark until 1533, when a monk named Negus Lebna Dengel spirited the *tabot* (i.e., the ark of the covenant) to safety just prior to Gragn's arrival.[7] Wherever it went, I am told, it stayed for about one hundred years until the danger had passed and then returned to Axum's newly constructed *second* St. Mary of Zion Church.

Birani led us back to the center of the compound until we stood at the spot I had long imagined. Between the two imposing churches, just above the ruins of the original St. Mary of Zion, sat the chapel of the holy ark. Standing there in person seemed unreal. Beside the chapel's sturdy, red-spiked fence, an especially well-robed retinue of monks hunched down, bowed in prayer. Of all the holy places we had seen this day, I knew this modest chapel exceeded them all. Somewhere inside its thick, cinder-block walls sat what locals believe is the original ark of the covenant.

For several minutes we stood in the afternoon shadows, staring speechless at the building. *Could it be true? Did I now stand less than twenty yards from the ark, the sign of the covenant made between God and his chosen people, Israel?*

Joby whispered, as if reminding himself, "This is it; this is where the ark is said to rest."

Like Joby, all I could do was stare, clench-jawed, soaking in the mystique of a place neither of us could fully comprehend. Birani left us alone. Words couldn't capture the moment, so he didn't try.

Six

MEN IN WHITE

The first thin rays of another blistering day peaked over the horizon, shining through my window at the Yeha Hotel. I rose, got dressed, and went to wake Jody for the day's business. Yet a melodic noise in the valley below drew me back down the hillside, along a flight of stone steps to a rock strewn footpath, where I sidled in with a chanting throng of praying pilgrims. They marched in rhythm through the streets of Axum. In the bracing predawn chill, I decided to join in, momentarily hiding myself in the crowd, wrestling to separate the subtle artifices of history from the elusive strands of truth.

Suddenly, the prayer line engulfed me and seemed to fill the streets to overflowing. I found myself surrounded by thousands of worshipers walking in smooth, swaying rhythms, wrapped in dingy white linens and chanting beautiful Ethiopian hymns.

I kept in step the best I could, capturing the scene on video, trying to blend in. I hadn't imagined such a lavish pageant as this and quickly decided that Sundays in Axum feature an intensity of prayer and devotion rarely encountered anywhere else. The pilgrims swept me up in their rapturous ritual, welcomed me to their citywide day of homage and contrition. This rising, swelling, almost hypnotic procession moved gracefully through the streets toward the rustic chapel.

By joining in the Sunday morning revelry, I saw firsthand the penetrating influence of Ethiopian Orthodoxy. Observing the role and status of the saints allowed me to see how something as symbolically profound as the holy ark, though never intended to be revered or worshiped, might have evolved into something else.

As we wound our way through town, the undulating assembly filled the stone-walled courtyard of St. Mary of Zion. Several dozen monks in long, flowing vestments and ornate, velvet robes entered the church. The rest of us remained outside, pressed against the outer wall.

Here, walking arm in arm with the softly chanting Axumites, I felt totally at peace. No one seemed to notice me or care that I'd imposed myself upon their holy rite. Making brief eye contact with children and adults I beheld only shy smiles and warm invitations. They seemed flattered I would even attempt to join their worship ceremony.

I can't say how long it took, but the group finally broke up, and individuals started marching. I took the moment to hurry back to the Yeha to retrieve Joby, who had just finished breakfast. He said he'd watched some of the pageant from the rear terrace over morning coffee.

"Man, Bubba, they rise early for church here. All that singing and praying woke me up."

I shoved the video camera in his hand and said, "Let's go!" As we hurried back down the hill, we met Birani, waiting for us at the edge of the compound. Together we rejoined the marchers just as the priests reemerged from the chapel, pumping prayer sticks overhead. They now wore elaborate red, purple, and green robes edged in silver with gold and red piping; behind them trailed long, bejeweled amulets embroidered in technicolor shades of fine silk. Some thrust red brocaded umbrellas aloft, while everywhere white-robed peasants whirled and sang, playing ten-stringed *begenas* and shaking *sistras*, an ancient Ethiopian instrument of metal disks that emits a rattling jingle.

Finally the pilgrims began circling the church in slow, surging waves—seven times, Birani pointed out—in memory of the Israelites marching around Jericho. With Joby shooting footage, I joined in, swaying and stutter-stepping in staccato time. Afterward, we all sat down to another three hours of praying and singing. By early afternoon, as a searing sun left even the most energetic worshipers glassy-eyed and wilted, the crowd began to disperse to attend neighborhood feasts and saint-day celebrations.

When I found Joby, a glow shone about his face as if he'd just emerged from a Baptist tent revival. We both realized that, cultural differences aside, we shared something important with these people. As alien as their ways struck us, they worshiped and adored Jesus nonetheless. Jesus died for these humble folk just as he died for us—the only difference being, so far as I could tell, that while Americans race off to brunch after church, these diligent disciples stand and march and sing and pray for five hours. It's the same cross, the same Savior, even if everything else looked and felt like another religion.

As the crowd thinned, Birani reappeared. "The high priests have agreed to meet with you. Come, if you are ready."

PRIESTS OF THE COVENANT

Anyone who wants to enter an Ethiopian church must first remove his or her shoes. As we entered the little side building across the courtyard from the chapel, Birani instructed us to remove our footwear.

The small, dilapidated building, overlooking the trench where the original St. Mary of Zion Cathedral once stood, contained only one long splintered table and a few folding metal chairs. The walls had been painted a gaudy, cartoon-sky blue; and the priests, all looking older than dirt, sat across the room, staring at us in their ceremonial white robes.

Birani handled the introductions, then we all sat down—Joby, Birani, and I facing a hastily convened tribunal. Out of deference to their white robes, I'd worn a starched white shirt, buttoned to the top. The priests, five of them, sat silent for a long time, watching us. One, named Narud, turned out to be the leader. Tall and slender even sitting in his chair, Narud had a pleasant, thinly bearded face and large, sparkling eyes. His long, ceremonial robe looked identical to those worn by the priests at the morning pageant; suspended about his neck hung a large, ornate wooden crucifix. As we spoke, he calmly massaged a pale green lime in his left hand.

My first question, unfortunately, betrayed my poor sense of protocol: "May we please meet the guardian of the ark?" I blurted out. Birani winced. The priests shook their heads, embarrased, casting side glances at one another. Narud rubbed his beard in quiet chagrin. I sensed my affront but as yet had no feel for the culture. What did they expect of foreign guests? Did they want me to *pay* for the privilege? Birani, shifting uneasily, began to translate, but needn't have bothered.

"Many have come before you, asking the same questions," Narud said sternly. "All but a few have been turned away."

Acknowledging my error, I nervously spoke another awkward question: "Has anyone but the guardian ever *seen* the ark?"

Narud exhaled patiently, while the others squirmed in their chairs. Narud finally spoke, his heavily accented English quite passable. Still he motioned for Birani to translate.

"Nobody," he began, "but the guardian is allowed access to the ark. A chosen few may have stood in the presence of the ark, but of these matters I cannot speak. This is as it should be. Neither will the world see it or photograph it or touch it—*ever!* It is forbidden." His impassive face turned severe. "*We* are entrusted with guarding the ark of the covenant," he continued, placing the lime on the table. "It is our sacred commission to conceal its powers and protect its holiness."

The other priests sat in quiet deference to Narud, and I quickly came to understand that this judiciary eldership served as the official buffer and first line of defense for the ark's guardian. In the minute it had taken Narud to answer my first two questions, I also saw they possessed an unshakable belief that the sacred relic—the authentic ark of the covenant, constructed at the foot of Mount Sinai to contain the tablets of stone and bearing the authentic Ten Commandments—now resided in their humble monastery. Narud explained that, in addition to this priestly order, the entire population—including members of the church and all Christian peoples of Tigray—considered it their birthright to protect the holy ark. If by some foolhardy stroke some foreign band of mercenaries or government invasion force ever dared to storm Axum and tried to steal the ark, the intruders would experience the savage side of these gentle villagers, who would gladly die in its defense, baring their teeth and wielding machetes.

I changed my approach. "Does the ark still have its powers?" I asked.

Narud leaned back. "Yes," he said, "but it is not the power of the ark that matters to us. In the teaching of the Ethiopian Orthodox Church, God is the reigning King, the only source of power in the universe, the One and only Creator of all existing life." He lifted his arms. "God himself is our source, and he alone possesses light and power and grace."

I nodded in agreement, though I wanted to mention that this seemed to contradict the practice of women praying to the ark for blessing. Then, with a smile, Narud acknowledged the true intent of my question, softly explaining what he understood to be the undeniable relationship between God, the ark, and his people.

"Since the ark, even today, contains the ten sacred words of the Law, written by God," he said, "the gift of his holiness cannot be diminished within it." He paused, then added, "Yes, it is true. Today his grace still rests upon the ark. It remains holy and significant."

Turning to Birani for support, I asked, "Does this mean that the ark still manifests the powers described in the Bible?" The question set the priests to murmering. Birani had, only a day earlier, alluded to the ark's powers, describing how barren women are made able to conceive under its divine influence. Still, I had something more in mind. I had learned of unconfirmed reports of the ark manifesting powers similar to those described in the Book of Exodus. Some suggested that former rulers of Ethiopia had not only believed in the ark's undiminished powers but had, as in the days of Joshua, employed the relic in battle. And in certain cases, it was said, it provided not merely a source of spiritual strength but raw, overcoming power against foreign aggressors.[1]

One such incident reportedly occurred as recently as 1896, when, at the Battle of Adowa in the Tigray region, Ethiopian King Menelik II confronted a well-armed battalion of Italian invaders. Intent on colonizing the whole country, the Italians converged on the Abyssinian highlands from the Eritrean coastal strip and attacked Menelik, who, eyewitnesses insist, had instructed the priests to carry the ark of the covenant onto the battlefield. Newspaper accounts of the battle report that Menelik was victorious against the eighteen thousand well-equipped, heavily armed Italians under the command of

General Baratieri. Menelik's comparatively ill-prepared and poorly armed troops went into battle at Adowa on the morning of March 1 and within six hours recorded a staggering victory—described by one historian as "the most notable victory of an African over a European army since the time of Hannibal."[2]

If nothing else, such sensational reports added a layer of luster to the Ethiopian legend. And while it makes for an intriguing bit of speculation, the monastery priests sitting across the table from me didn't care to discuss it. Either they didn't know of such reports, or they chose to conceal them. I could hardly blame them. From their perspective, I amounted to little more than a pesky interloper asking impertinent questions. I could see my challenge would be to change their perception.

Still, their silence left me wondering: if the ark had indeed retained its powers, how might it be used today? Some commentators theorized that the rebel TPLF (Tigray People's Liberation Front), which fought so effectively against overwhelmingly superior government forces to gain control of Axum in 1991, might also have benefitted from the ark's powers.[3] Though fascinating to ponder, without corroborating evidence it reads like a fable (not unlike the queen of Sheba folklore), inspired by some politico to add a scintillating paragraph or two to the national epic.

I recall thinking: *Why would the ark still have power today? Hadn't the veil been torn in the temple? Didn't Christ on the cross say, "It is finished," effectively ending the old covenant? And wouldn't that have emptied the ark of power? Had these tales of some mysterious, abiding power of the ark grown more fantastic with each retelling, like grandpa telling fish stories over the years; the fish get bigger each time the story is told?*

Before we left, I asked Narud to describe the ark. He held up his hand and said, "As it has been for the last thousand

61

years, so it will be for the next thousand. How it is described in the Bible, so it is today."

By his tone I realized our interview had ended.

Joby and I stood and thanked the priests, and with many smiles and handshakes we pulled out a bag of medicine—antibiotics, aspirin, antiseptic creams, adhesive bandages—that I had packed as a goodwill offering. Then I handed Birani $100 in Ethiopian birr and asked him to tell the priests they should use it to buy tea (Birani had mentioned that the monks love tea and would drink it continuously if they had money to buy it). Last, I gave each man a watch as a final show of gratitude.

They seemed grateful but maintained their hard countenances toward us. I hadn't often experienced such steely indifference, even in closed Muslim cultures, where everyone, it seemed, had their price, and where most roadblocks could be negotiated with a bit of charm and ingenuity. Here the monks expressed not the slightest interest in money or gifts (one even told me he couldn't take an aspirin for his headache because he was fasting) or in sharing their secret with the world. When I asked how they expected the world to believe they had the ark, they responded with looks of boredom. They had no use for publicity and didn't care whether the world knew anything of the ark's true whereabouts. They had no intention of divulging their secret, and my questions had become tiresome.

TEMPLE TREASURE

The LORD said to Moses: "Make two trumpets of hammered silver, and use them for calling the community together and for having the camps set out" (Num. 10:1–2).

As we turned to leave, Birani lifted a hand. The priests had, after some discussion, decided to show Joby and me a sampling of the treasures stored within St. Mary of Zion. The church basement, he explained, served as a vast repository of the priceless crowns of former Ethiopian rulers, as well as many other "archaeological wonders" too rare for public display.

We thanked the priests again and followed Birani across the courtyard to the high iron fence at the rear of the chapel. As we waited, I inspected its well-fortified ramparts. The rear courtyard had been built like a military bunker with thick, reinforced, cinder-block walls framing a big walk-out basement.

"There," said Birani, "is where the temple treasures are kept."

I scanned the back wall of the chapel, hoping for a glimpse of the guardian. I'd been told he strolled the grounds inside the fence and occasionally poked his head out of a window or a side door. After fifteen minutes a smartly bearded temple guard wearing a bright yellow robe, a white turban, and funky Ray-ban sunglasses (that he no doubt had obtained from a tourist) emerged from the darkened walk-out. He strode to the fence to a long, canvas-covered box, perched on a metal-frame platform painted with yellow primer.

"This is the temple treasurer," Birani said, whispering. The treasurer nodded, then opened a door on the side of the box, lifting it to reveal a stunning exhibit of gold and silver crowns. They all sat side by side, sporting the ornate royal crests of former Ethiopian rulers (I found it comical that these precious crowns sat on a worn, flower-print tablecloth.)

Each crown seemed an intricate, jewel-encrusted work of medieval art, topped by elaborate silver crosses and miniature gold replicas of the sacred *tabot*. I looked up. The treasurer had departed. "Where did he go?" I asked Birani.

"He will return," he replied with sparkle in his eye. "He has something else to show you, something you might find interesting."

After several minutes the treasurer returned, carrying two long instruments, bound tightly in linen. I thought at first they might be ancient muskets, perhaps used in one of Tigray's civil wars. But then I noted their indescribably old and tarnished appearance; looking closer, I recognized them as hammered silver trumpets. The treasurer held them out for our brief inspection, then lay them alongside the crowns. Yes, these long-necked trumpets, with rich engravings and ceremonial design, clearly belonged among Axum's imperial treasures. I could have sworn I'd seen them or their likenesses somewhere, but I couldn't recall where.

Birani interpreted while the treasurer explained: "These trumpets have great value to Ethiopian Orthodoxy. They are the original ceremonial trumpets from the first temple in Jerusalem." I swallowed hard while he added: "Our tradition confirms it. Our ancestors recorded in their records that the trumpets arrived in Ethiopia, along with the other temple vessels, from Jerusalem. They came in Menelik's caravan with the ark of the covenant."

I stood speechless, weighing his words, staring blankly at the heavily oxidized instruments—nearly five feet long and wrapped heavily in rags. The treasurer said they had been forged of hammered silver, but they had a smoky, almost bronzed appearance, so pitted and tarnished they had grown from age and exposure. Suddenly I recalled where I'd seen their twins: these battered trumpets appeared identical, both in size and appearance, to a pair I'd seen carved into the Arch of Titus in Rome. That arch commemorated Titus's destruction of Jerusalem in A.D. 70, described by Jewish historian Flavius Josephus as a sacking so thorough that even the walls and foundations of the street had been destroyed: "It was so thoroughly laid even with the ground by those that dug it up to the foundation, that there was left nothing to make those that came thither believe it had ever been inhabited."[4]

Titus removed from the second temple Judaism's sacred vessels and treasures, then paraded them through the streets of Rome during a victory celebration. These included the golden menorah, the showbread table, and, of course, the silver trumpets, memorialized in 2 Chronicles 13:12: "God is with us; he is our leader. His priests with their trumpets will sound the battle cry against you. Men of Israel, do not fight against the LORD, the God of your fathers, for you will not succeed."

Though Titus had despoiled the second temple, it made sense that the trumpets and vessels he took would be exact copies of those from the first temple. That meant that the long-necked trumpets carved into the Arch of Titus in Rome would match the appearance and dimensions of the first temple trumpets. Recall the words of the Lord to Moses: "Make two trumpets of hammered silver, and use them for calling the community together and for having the camps set out" (Num. 10:1–2).

I could hardly believe it. Sitting on a table, not four feet away, appeared to be, at least, the identical twins of the trumpets described in Numbers.

I turned to Joby. "Did you hear *that?*"

He nodded, duly impressed but unsure how to respond. Could these tarnished old trumpets be the same as those forged in Old Testament days and placed by Solomon in the first temple? When I pressed the guard for more details, he refused to elaborate. As with so many other so-called "facts" of Ethiopian heritage, the truth of the matter remained (at least for the moment) clouded.

I had come to Ethiopia searching for answers, but my list of questions had only grown. As we returned across the courtyard toward the hotel, Birani revealed that the basement of the old church held thousands of other implements, relics, crowns, and vessels, all cataloged by ancient curators.

For my first trip to this bizarre corner of the world, I had stumbled onto ancient treasures that seemed like bread crumbs along a fog-covered trail. I'd already accepted that I would not be granted permission, on this trip at least, to meet the guardian of the ark. That honor would have to come later. Still, I wanted more.

Suddenly I felt an urge to visit one last sacred landmark: Tana Kirkos Island on the mysterious Lake Tana, some two hundred miles to the south. According to tradition, this holy island had served as the hiding place of the ark of the covenant for more than eight hundred years. I had seen the chapel of the ark, met with the high monks, and inspected "temple treasures." Now, before I left, I had to try to see this island with my own eyes.

Unfortunately, other tourists we had met in Axum said they had tried in vain to see Tana Kirkos. They had begged their travel agents, pled with local government officials, even petitioned the Ethiopian Ministry of Tourism, but had been resolutely barred from visiting the island. Something about it remained off-limits to foreigners. The reports didn't bode well for us.

Ecuba had rejoined us outside the gate, having arranged for us to visit other historic sites in the area.

"Ecuba," I said with scarcely tempered excitement. "I want to go to Tana Kirkos Island. Can you make that happen?"

Ecuba stared at me. He paused, then bowed politely. "I will see what can be done." With that he turned and raced back toward the Yeha Hotel.

SEVEN

LAND BEYOND THE RIVERS

When I returned to the hotel, Ecuba already had used the phone at the front desk. "I have called my good friend Misgana Genanew," he said, "in Bahar Dar."

I knew Bahar Dar. It sat on the southern shore of Lake Tana, precisely where I hoped to travel.

Ecuba seemed excited to declare his news. "You can fly to Bahar Dar today, and Misgana will meet you," he said. "He will be able to get permission for you to go to Tana Kirkos."

It sounded great but didn't seem to make much sense. A day earlier a group of French tourists had irritably informed us that they'd tried everything since their arrival to get permission to visit Lake Tana, but their pleas had fallen on deaf ears. They had received neither luck nor cooperation from anyone with the authority to grant their request. Now Ecuba was telling us our visit already had been arranged, that his enterprising friend Misgana, who worked for a Bahar Dar-based travel company called Jacaranda Tours, would handle everything.

"Misgana knows the minister of tourism," Ecuba explained. Then, smiling, he assured us, "With Misgana, sailing to Tana Kirkos will pose no problem. He will arrange your passage."

Suddenly I couldn't wait to meet this Misgana fellow; he seemed to be well-connected. Braced by Ecuba's encouraging news, Joby and I hastily packed and said good-bye to Birani. I had grown fond of the retired monk in our short time together. He had gently and patiently taken us under his wing, asked little in return, and ushered us unexpectedly into the rarefied realm of Axum's priestly order. Moreover, he had shared personal insights into the nature and ways of the ark among the Axumites and imparted a solid understanding of the ark's role in Ethiopian Orthodoxy. Through him, I had gained new perspective into Axum's mystique, witnessing firsthand how legend and myth had blurred the history of Ethiopia. More importantly, old Birani treated me like a son. I thanked him profusely, and paid him handsomely, for his warm patience and kind tutelage.

Ecuba sped us out of Axum to the airport where we bought tickets for the one-hour flight to Bahar Dar. After a short wait a twin-engine Fokker-50 prop plane dropped out of the sky, rumbled to a stop among the grazing cattle, and opened its doors. We grabbed our bags and hopped aboard, bracing ourselves as the plane blasted down the rocky runway, lifted off over the crimson cliffs, and buzzed us south, past the Takazee River, with its web of canyons and tributaries slicing the countryside into slivers of silver and scarlet.

Within minutes the terrain below shifted from arid high desert to a countryside dark and green. When we landed at Bahar Dar's comparatively modern, asphalt-paved airport, we stepped into a thick curtain of humidity. The air reeked of burning rubbish, and our shirt collars instantly turned damp, while a film of sweat rose on our faces and foreheads. We retrieved our bags in the terminal and found ourselves face-to-face with a lanky, smiling Ethiopian.

"Hello, Mr. Bob?" he began, "I am Misgana. It is a pleasure to meet you. I have made all the arrangements for your trip to Lake Tana. Please," he added with a deferential bow, "come with me."

I found his manner amiable but his assurances implausible. I followed him to the cab, hoping our young guide could back up his words. Talking and laughing and asking us questions about our adventures in Axum, Misgana hopped in the front seat next to the cabby and immediately began pointing out Bahar Dar's finer points. He called attention to its beautiful streets and cobblestone plazas, overflowing with enormous clay planters filled with black and red orchids and sprays of dayglow azaleas. Bahar Dar looked and felt like a seaside port, which, given the enormity of Lake Tana mere blocks away, it may as well have been. Driving along its shady, cobbled lanes, bordered pleasantly with jacaranda and flame trees, I noted the neat rows of plush palms hanging over the roadways, like tasseled lamp shades casting dark, cooling shadows.

"Now *this* is Africa," I said to Joby, who sat staring blissfully out the passenger window, pointing out monkeys rollicking in the treetops and trying to identify the long-beaked, tropical birds whooping it up atop the swaying jacaranda. En route, Misgana filled us in: his good friend, Gebeyehu (pronounced Gubar-you) Wogawehu, worked for the Tourism and Information Department in Bahar Dar and had granted us permission to visit Tana Kirkos Island.

"You're kidding," I said.

"No," Misgana replied, "but there is one condition: Gebeyehu must accompany us and oversee our journey."

"No problem," I answered, less concerned with who joined us so long as we could sail out to the island. For reasons unexplained the Lake Tana region remained politically sensitive,

69

and foreign contact with the monks on the island had to be closely monitored. I didn't argue; rather, I felt enormously relieved that our visit had been sanctioned by the appropriate local governing body, thereby removing any temptation to take matters into my own hands.

"These days," Misgana interjected, "it is not often that we get requests from foreigners to visit Lake Tana's holy islands. It is why a government agent must travel along to make sure no customs are violated or artifacts stolen. The islands contain many treasures."

I nodded, deeply intrigued, while Misgana added: "You will also have to pay Gebeyehu's salary because he will have to take two days off of work."

It sounded fair to me—amounting probably to no more than a few hundred birr. I turned to Joby, who, peering up at the monkeys, drawled lazily, "Like my daddy said, 'If you want to dance, you've got to pay the fiddler.'"

SMOKING WATER

The remainder of the afternoon we spent visiting the famous Blue Nile Falls, some thirty miles inland from Bahar Dar into the rugged countryside. Traveling a bumpy, rutted road through dense forests, coarse fields, and rolling hills, we finally arrived at a dusty village called Tissisat, or "Water that Smokes"—a dark and dirty affair straight out of a 1950s Tarzan movie.

The place recalled my childhood image of Africa as a vine-filled jungle populated by primitive tribes and filled with mud-and-thatch huts. Milling about the mercado, some villagers sported enormous clay plates in their lips while others wore big earrings in lobes stretched thin as rubber bands. The village had a dark, oppressive feel: soot-covered artisans feverishly worked their crude bellows, hunched over smoldering fire pits next to piles of fresh-cut timber, hammering out razor-edged spearheads and knife-points on stone anvils.

As we drove along the crowded center corridor, congested with children, dogs, and chickens, I eyed a smattering of mud huts filled with a wondrous array of multicolored, blue, yellow, and red robes and shawls.

We paid for our tickets at a mud hutch beside an entry gate to the falls. I pulled out my wallet and immediately a little monkey, tethered to a rope, raced out from the shadows and snatched two birr—the exact price of admission—from my fingers. The monkey turned, stopped, and reached back, grabbing one more birr. Then it scampered back to its owner, who issued our passes to the Blue Nile Falls. Joby couldn't believe his eyes: "Hey, Bob," he laughed, "that monkey must be from Washington, D.C."

The rocky course to the falls led us through a dry patchwork of fields to a massive stone bridge spanning a small gorge. The Portuguese built the bridge in the early seventeenth century, Misgana said, and though it looked feeble from centuries of fierce rebel warfare, relentless sun, and other harsh elements, he assured us it still stood sturdy.

The humidity and heat pressed down on us. We climbed the opposite slope of the ravine, up a dusty hillside peopled by friendly artisans huddled under colorful tarpaulins. Most sold a high-quality, native jewelry fashioned over smoky fire pits from bits of red-hot metal. We negotiated the winding course into a thick mantle of tropical shrubbery. Nearing the crest, we began to feel underfoot a low, thundering vibration.

"Do you feel that?" Joby asked.

Atop the rise we stepped into a heavy, cool mist. I stared across the lush valley at an immense plume of white water hurling itself over a spectacular basalt cliff, filling the valley below with towering clouds of vapor. I could see where Tissisat got its name: the water truly seemed to be erupting in smoke.

Joby and I stood speechless before the endless waves of mist that reflected, in the yellow-pink sky, a kaleidoscope of rainbows. All about us grew a thick flora—not unlike a prehistoric rain forest—with monkeys howling overhead and the cool blast from the falls caressing our faces. For just a moment it felt as if we had traveled back in time to the beginning of life itself.

We hiked into the valley and crossed a narrow stream near the base of the falls where another huddle of boys, some blowing flutes and singing chirpy African songs, helped tourists wade across the gurgling stream. Huffing back up the facing slope, we reached the bank of a wide, slow-moving river, some two hundred yards above the boiling falls. A young man paddled over to us on a soggy *ambatch,* a bulky reed canoe lashed together with rope and reminiscent of those sailing Egypt's upper Nile. He motioned for us to hop aboard. Unstable as they might look, these high-prowed vessels are amazingly sturdy and regularly ply these waters while weighed down with several cows at a time. We paid the pilot a couple of birr to paddle us into the middle of the river and across to the other side. I counted it a minor thrill to be floating so close to the fall's roaring drop-off, but this young man had paddled across thousands of times and maneuvered us effortlessly across.

These majestic falls, and the Blue Nile itself, wind east, then south, then ramble north, carrying life and fertility through the Sudan to Egypt's Nile delta. Fed by enormous Lake Tana—a body of water six thousand feet above sea level and covering a surface area of 3,673 square miles—both the Blue and White Niles engorge during Ethiopia's long rainy season, flooding the Blue Nile northward into Egypt. This surge from Lake Tana and its network of rivers carries the nutrients and loam responsible for the Nile Delta's remarkable fertility. The bonds connecting these lands are as old as time.

Gazing back toward the river, my mind struck on a verse I'd recently read in Zephaniah 3:10: "From beyond the rivers of

Cush my worshipers, my scattered people, will bring me offerings." I took in the rich, fertile plateau, crisscrossed by rivers and streams made lush from heavy rains and humid skies, and realized, in all likelihood, I had arrived in the biblical land of Cush.

What else could lie beyond the rivers of Cush but the ancient Axumite kingdom? Pondering the phrase, "my worshipers . . . will bring me *offerings*," I recalled how, in some translations, the phrase read, "my worshipers shall bring My *gift*." As I admired the lush river basin, hazy from the spray of a million tons of water per second pounding the rocks below, I wondered: *Might this land of raging rivers one day render back to its rightful homeland the ultimate offering, the incomparable gift of the holy ark?*

Eight

HOLY LAKE, SACRED ISLAND

For sheer fun and adventure, few things compare with setting out on a vast body of water in the predawn chill.

It would require at least three and one-half hours by motorboat over Lake Tana's gently lapping, azure-green waves to reach Tana Kirkos Island. It lies like a humpback alligator sunning in a swamp, completely secluded in an enormous body of water rightly termed an inland sea.

Our government-appointed guide, Gebeyehu Wogawehu, met us at the pier at about 5:30 A.M. We leased a lightweight, aluminum-hulled skiff, designed to hold four people, and set off into the foggy dark.

Happy, buoyant Gebeyehu had short hair and a round face and wore a bulky green jacket which he refused to shed, even when the sun seared hot over both land and water. Like Misgana, Gebeyehu proudly called himself an Ethiopian Orthodox Christian, and while I knew he had been assigned to keep an eye on us, he never *acted* official; rather, he remained friendly, always eager to assist and answer our questions.

Once on the water Joby threw down his pack and parked himself along the railing near the bow, alternately napping and staring into the mist. I sat on a wooden bench on the stern, flushed with the romance of our journey and braced by the crisp morning coolness. A mile or two from shore, we passed a ragged flotilla of fishermen in their reed longboats. A large, blood-orange sun rose slowly on the horizon, while the sky filled with squawking seagulls and Egyptian geese skimming the water for insects.

76

Less than an hour into our journey, I lost sight of shore. Gazing into the glimmering rays of dawn and seeing nothing but water, I thought, *What a perfect place to hide the ark.*

I'd heard that as many as forty-five inhabited islands lay scattered across the lake. This mighty body of water, sur-rounded by dense, mountainous jungle, would've posed a formidable obstacle for a force looking to recapture the ark. Even in modern times, with motorized boats and modern nav-igational charts, it felt as though we were sailing into an uncharted ocean. No one, save the Tana natives and a handful of guides, had a clue where most of the islands lay. Where would one even *begin* to look on such a lake? Without a guide familiar with its remote reaches—or some inside access to Tana's monastic cultures—the ark's resting place would remain a watertight secret.

North African historians make a fair case that the ark had, in times of great peril, been whisked out of Axum and hidden in any number of secret places. The Muslim invasions of Ahmed Gragn, for instance—the aggressor who overran Tigray and nearly wiped Axum off the map—and Queen Gudit's car-nage in the tenth century, likely prompted the ark's caretakers to remove it to one hideout or another. The islands of Lake Tana have long been regarded as the hideout of choice,[1] but the question remains: *which* island?

Two stand out. Due west of Tana Kirkos lies an island called Daga Stephanos, today regarded as one of the holiest places on the sacred lake. Monks on Daga Stephanos have maintained a church monastery there for the past thousand years, and some believe the ark stayed there in times of distress. Today the island serves as the sepulcher of five former Ethiopian emperors, held perpetually in state in glass-encased crypts.

I decided to skip Daga Stephanos for two reasons: first, because there seemed to be no physical evidence to suggest the ark had ever been there; and second, its monks have a surly, combative reputation. They either feign ignorance of their island's heritage or choose to keep such information to themselves.[2]

Tana Kirkos, in my opinion, safeguards a tradition far more credible. For one, the monks there proudly report that the original ark once rested in a tabernacle on their island, for eight hundred years prior to its flight to Axum. Far more obliging than the Daga Stephanos order, these monks pointed Graham Hancock to an ancient altar high on a cliff, where they said blood sacrifices had been performed, near where the relic had once been tended. It had apparently been the object of Old Testament-style blood sacrifices and purification rites.[3] I wanted to meet the Tana Kirkos monks and hear their story.

As the sun rose over the lake, Misgana lay asleep on the narrow seat of the boat. He had grown up on one of Tana's islands and knew the lake like his own backyard. His father grew coffee beans, and the pair had often sailed from one island to the next, bartering at villages and visiting relatives.

"We never went to Tana Kirkos," Misgana said. "No one goes *there*."

Apparently the Tana Kirkos monks maintain a flourishing internal commerce—cultivating crops and coffee and operating as a closed religious sect—and have little motive for interisland trade. Two and one-half hours into our journey,

Misgana lifted his head, raised a hand, and mumbled, "There is Tana Kirkos."

SCENE OF THE CRIME

At a distance the island revealed little more than a few leafy trees breaking the surf, but the closer we floated, the larger it grew. It finally towered above us, its tall cliffs whiskered near the shore with thick foliage and crowned by leaning olive trees. Nearer still I could make out the outline of a small hutch standing atop one of the cliffs. It sat between alien-looking, menorah-shaped barrel cactus. Overhead circled three kingfishers scouting for Nile perch.

The captain steered the skiff into a shady lagoon. As he pulled close to the rocks, I saw a thin flight of granite steps chiseled into the cliff. After tying off, Misgana ushered Joby, Gebeyehu, and me onto the rocks and up the steps.

Joby and I left our camping gear on the boat. If the monks consented, we hoped to spend the night, though both Misgana and Gebeyehu cautioned us that no outsider, so far as they knew, had ever slept overnight on the island.

"I do not think the monks will allow it," Gebeyehu declared.

Still, if the opportunity presented itself, I wanted to be ready. We could use the extra time to poke around and see what curiosities might present themselves. My strategy was simple: let the island tell its story without any prompting.

Any decent investigation, of course, takes time. No one should enter a crime scene with a preset agenda. I had learned that lesson the hard way. When, as a rookie cop, I entered a house looking for a shell casing or a footprint, I nearly always missed other crucial evidence—like a tiny snip of clothing snagged to a screen door, or a fresh scrape of paint beneath a picture frame.

Graham Hancock had arrived on Tana Kirkos in a huff, distracted by the cost of his $50-per-hour charter cruise, and dealt rudely with the timid monks. With no patience for common courtesies or small talk, he never really got to tour the island. He interrogated the chief priest, recited a quick list of questions, hiked up to the altar, and left. Since so few outsiders had ever visited the island, I felt certain clues and evidence remained, probably well off the beaten path. I wanted to get to *know* these people and felt prepared to spend as much time with them as they would allow.

Yet within minutes of my arrival, my optimism vanished. Hiking down the narrow trail to meet us, Tana Kirkos' chief priest, in his loose, flowing white robe and turban, stopped us in our path. He strode up to Misgana and Gebeyehu and immediately began peppering them with questions. Lean, bearded, with a prayer shawl thrown backward over his shoulders, he seemed none too pleased to see us. After a few moments of heated discourse, Misgana backed away and whispered, "The village elder will not let you on the island if you are not an Orthodox Christian."

"What?" I asked, stupefied. I did a quick mental inventory: we'd paid for proper government approval, been granted security clearance. "I thought monks were open to visits by outsiders," I replied.

Misgana shrugged. "He wants to know if you are *Orthodox* Christians because there have been former visitors who didn't understand their spiritual beliefs and ways. They offended the monks with their rudeness and extravagant demands."

Though it had been almost ten years, I wondered if they meant Graham Hancock. I didn't know how to respond, but I certainly hadn't come this far to be turned away so quickly. I walked straight up to the priest and asked Misgana to translate.

"I am Bob Cornuke of the United States," I began, "and I am a Christian. I would like to come onto your island and learn more about your culture." Misgana relayed my message to the dispassionate monk, who answered in Amharic, staring straight into my eyes.

"He wants to know if you are an *Orthodox* Christian?" Misgana repeated.

"No, I am not," I replied, "but ask him this: When he says a prayer, does he pray in the name of the Orthodox Christian Church? Or to Jesus?"

Misgana translated, and the priest replied: "He says, 'to Jesus!'"

"Then tell him that we worship the same God. Though I am not of the Ethiopian Orthodox Church, I am a Christian who prays to Jesus. He is my Savior, which means *we*"—I pointed to the priest—"are Christian brothers. We are followers of the same Jesus."

I held out my hand. The priest hesitated, then smiled. After a moment Misgana turned and said, "Abba says you are welcome."

The priest, named Abba Baye (Abba for "father"), bowed slightly and approached me with an outstretched hand, shaking mine with his right hand while holding my wrist with his left—a gesture of honor and respect. We exchanged handshakes and hugs, and a lengthy greeting ensued, after which the priest led us up the overgrown path through a stone archway and into a grassy clearing. There we saw a couple of dilapidated shacks and a few raggedly dressed monks, the latter genuinely stunned to see us.

After a brief round of introductions, they led us higher up the path toward their village, which sat atop a hillside thick with scrub and alive with hummingbirds and starlings. We walked under a canopy of creeping vines. I looked up and jolted backward. Concealed among the thick, green mantle hung a curtain of spiderwebs crawling with dozens of black, fat-bellied, long-legged spiders, some larger than my fully outstretched hand.

"Are they poisonous?" Joby asked.

"Yes, they are poisonous," Misgana replied, "but they aren't aggressive. I have seen the monks let them crawl up their arms. They rarely bite."

I ducked under the webs, glancing up to see spiders scrambling in all directions. We continued up the path, finally reaching the village. The compound struck me as a depressingly glum affair—little more than a small circle of thatched huts, dirty and sunbaked and devoid of the remotest hint of creature comforts.

"Where are all the monks?" I asked.

"Most of the monks are still at work on the other side of the island," Misgana explained. "They tend the monastery's modest fields of teff, coffee, and vegetables."

I peered west and saw a marshy finger of land stretching away from the main island, connected to another half-submerged sliver of peninsula. From a distance I could just make out the bobbing white robes of monks toiling in the heat.

The ground about us lay strewn with dusty piles of unshucked coffee berries. A few small boys gathered about, leaning on sticks and dressed in tattered shorts, wrapped to their necks in heavy prayer shawls. They stared at us, perplexed.

Misgana led me to a small hutch, raised up on thick, lashed logs and set on hewn stones. He pulled open a thatch door to reveal a claustrophobic space that served as a monk's sleeping quarters. No larger than a file cabinet tipped on its side, its walls harbored nests of leggy spiders and other mites and insects. With no ventilation or windows, it struck me as the most austere living quarters I'd ever seen. In these bleak cubicles the monks slept and prayed and endured their monastic lives from childhood to death.

I didn't immediately ask about the ark, preferring instead to spend that first afternoon and evening mixing with the monks, watching their routine, eating when they ate, playing with the children, and, later, praying together in a dark, smoky hut that served as their church. Over the course of hours, I gained a feel of the rhythms of the village and sensed the chief priest warming up to me. Abba never asked us for money—a positive sign—and seemed to recognize we had no intention of pressing an agenda. The longer Abba considered it, the more he seemed to appreciate my bold confession of our mutual Savior.

Shortly before the evening meal, we met the rest of the order: a sweaty, dirty band of monks straggling into camp. One of them walked with a staff and a bad limp, the result of a huge wound oozing from his instep. It seemed he'd swung an axe a few weeks back, but instead of splitting a log, nearly hacked off his foot. He'd dislodged a two-inch wedge from his arch, the flesh split wide to reveal gray bone.

"Such injuries are common on the islands," Misgana explained, as we could clearly see by the sordid collection of discolored, swollen, deeply scarred legs and limbs before us. The poor fellow's foot had swollen to twice its normal size, and, with no medicine or antiseptic to fight the infection, the prognosis wasn't good. With the permission of the head priest, Joby and I took the poor fellow aside, cleansed and bandaged the wound, and administered a heavy dose of antibiotics. We gave him a month's supply of capsules—enough, we hoped, to wipe out the infection—along with instructions on how, and how many, to take.

After evening prayer services, the monks brought out another suffering soul, sprawled on a mat of palm fronds. This groaning old man had contracted a severe infection near a rather sensitive area between his legs. The pain had grown so intense that for days he hadn't been able to walk. I looked at

Joby, snatched a pair of rubber gloves and some topical antibi-
otic cream from my pack, and handed them to my friend.

"Joby, *here*," I said. "Put some of this on the infection."

Joby shot me a look as if I'd skinned his favorite hunting
dog. "What?" he whispered, glancing down at the pus-filled
ulceration between the fellow's thigh and buttocks.

"Yes," I nodded, having no intention of doing the deed
myself. "It's important. I know you can do it."

With a sigh Joby pulled on the rubber gloves and began
carefully, in the manner of a person handling rusty razor blades,
to clean and daub cream on the open sore.

"You owe me, Bubba! You owe me big!" he kept saying.
When he finally finished, the wound looked a little better. We
left the man still wincing, yet bowing and thanking us with
great sincerity.

CIRCUS KIRKOS

As I'd hoped, Abba decided to let us spend the night; Joby
and I could set up our tents on the cliff above the village.
Misgana said the privilege "should be regarded as a rare honor."

As it had been for the last one thousand years, the monks
turned in at dusk. They would rise, as always, by 4:00 A.M. for
prayers. Joby and I gathered our gear and hiked to the highest
point of the island, pitching camp on a sheer spine of ridge
barely wide enough to support our tent. In these compact quarters, merely rolling over in our sleep might send us hurling off
a cliff into the lagoon. So we cleared the area of leaves and
placed a ring of stones around our tent to wake us should we
begin to roll.

An African moon, surreal and luminous, shone down on
the island, reflecting eerily in the lapping tide below. From our
perch I could just make out the thin outline of the marshy
peninsula across the cove. A deep indigo sky shimmered with
stars.

Soon I noticed a mild buzzing; then it grew louder, incessant. By rustling the leaves on this ancient cliff, we had stirred thousands of creeping and winged insects from their ancient nests. By the fury of their response, it appeared they had enjoyed relatively quiet and undisturbed lives among the thistles and cracks—until our arrival. Within minutes, Joby and I found ourselves under full assault, beset by a plague of stinging bugs and mosquitoes of a size and temperament I'd never encountered. The mosquitoes came at us in angry, stinging clouds. To counter the attack, Joby and I slathered ourselves with an entire bottle of mosquito repellent, then started a small fire atop the ridge.

With the insects temporarily at bay, we sat back and embraced the moment. A fresh breeze blew in off the lake, and a small bank of clouds misted across the moon. The dark skies dazzled now with stars brighter than diamonds, and Lake Tana—black, sullen, immense—seemed to mingle with the heavenly expanse. Surrounded by palm fronds enveloped in soft trickles of smoke, it seemed as if I'd been edited into a Johnny Weismuller movie. I half expected to see Boy stroll into camp with Cheetah in hand; and sure enough, as I stirred the fire, I looked up to see a row of white eyes staring at us through the canopy of black. Curious monks, no doubt, had come up to spy on the crazy Americans.

I waved them in, and, after several moments, one of the bolder ones tiptoed to the edge of our makeshift camp—a boy, no more than fourteen years old, probably apprenticing from a nearby island. I stood up. He jumped back, startled by my quick movement.

"Joby, hand me a candy bar," I whispered. Joby rummaged in his pack and pulled out a piece of chocolate. I handed it to the boy, motioning for him to take a bite.

"Joby, show him how to chew it."

Joby took an exaggerated bite of a candy bar, prompting the lad to chomp into the Snickers, wrapper and all. Not only had these island dwellers never seen a candy bar, but they also had no idea what to make of a wrapper. In slow motion I walked over and unwrapped the candy. The young man took a nibble, then a bite. After he swallowed, a smile crossed his face. Suddenly six other boys—all between fourteen and eighteen years of age—leaped out from the darkness. All wanted Snickers bars.

The older monks had gone to bed; the night belonged to the young. After endless nights of prayer and eating alone and candles out by 7:30 P.M., they acted as if the circus had come to town. Joby and I handed out more candy and watched, amused, as the boys gobbled it up. After a strict diet of vegetables and sour *injera*, that first bite of chocolate must've tasted like heaven. Unfortunately, young, pure bodies unaccustomed to sugar soon began bounding about the ridge like kids on Christmas morning.

Joby took out our two-way radio and turned it on. After a short demonstration two boys started shouting at each other through the radios, scurrying about the ridge. I took out my night-vision binoculars and showed them how to see into the dark. Seconds later they had commandeered the binoculars and taken them over to the cliff, where, peering down into the village, they began giggling uncontrollably. I strolled over to see that they had undertaken a bit of island espionage, watching the older monks coming and going from the village outhouse. Soon the boys began laughing out loud, fighting one another for the binoculars, and viewing with hilarity proceedings that had, until that moment, remained private.

"Joby," I said, "what have we done?"

The boys were now running amok. Prior to our arrival, Tana Kirkos had experienced twenty-five hundred years of uninterrupted solitude. Now, laughing boys buzzing from sugar and bewitched by fancy gadgets ran through the jungle as if drunk on moonshine. In one brief interchange, I feared, we had unraveled centuries of religious tradition. I turned to Joby, who was sitting back and watching the youthful antics with a mixture of delight and concern.

"Joby," I whispered, ducking sparks as one boy tripped over the fire pit while screaming into a radio, "it took them twenty-five hundred years to build this unique island culture, and we've managed to wreck it in twenty minutes."

Πἰπε

TEMPLE VESSELS

"Bong! Bong! Bong!"

Prying my eyes awake, I squinted at my watch—4:30 A.M., under a jet black sky. With only a few Yemen fireflies circling in front of the flap, I crawled from our tent, shuffled over to the cliff, and looked down to see a young monk clobbering a spent .50 caliber artillery shell with a fat stick. Someone had hung a rusty Russian casing by a string to use as a dinner/wake-up bell. Aside from a sooty cooking pot down by the village, it was the first refined metal I'd seen on the island. A soldier, no doubt (perhaps one who grew up on one of the islands), had dropped it off from the mainland.

I shook Joby awake. We'd been invited to attend the monks' morning prayer service and needed to move quickly. I inspected our camp and saw a few wadded-up candy wrappers stuck in some bushes, the only proof of the previous night's chaos. Our two-way radios, slightly worse for wear, lay intact on opposite sides of camp; the night-vision binoculars, smudged with soot, had been abandoned next to the campfire pit.

Last evening's riotous events had come to a swift halt not twenty minutes after they began, when an elder monk appeared on the ridge. Framed in moonlight and regarding with astonishment a scene he'd probably never conceived, he barked an order in Amharic, freezing the youngsters in their tracks. Suddenly mute, they scrambled off the ridge into the village and shut themselves in their Spartan sleeping hutches. In seconds the island turned stone silent. Joby and I both groaned, relieved that no disaster had occurred as a result of our meddling. I prayed we had violated no sacred customs.

Morning came with soothing jungle sounds: island birds cawing, kingfishers swooshing overhead, brisk lake breezes rustling the trees. The wind drafting off the vast lake reminded me of the Rocky Mountains after a morning rain, and I fought off a pang of homesickness. Journeying so far from home, under such unpredictable circumstances, I often ask myself why I *do* this—and am ever thankful that I always seem to make it back.

Although I hadn't slept soundly, I felt energized and excited. Joby and I pulled on our boots, damp with dew and teeming with bugs, then padded our way down to the village. The monks already had begun to file into a small mud hut. Misgana strolled into camp, sleepy-eyed from his night on the boat. I told him what had happened on the ridge, and he just laughed.

Gebeyehu Wogawehu stood nearby in his green jacket, smiling: "Did you enjoy your camp-out, gentlemen?" I nodded, thinking that, for a government-appointed chaperon, Gebeyehu had been all but invisible.

One of the boys from the previous evening stood smartly at the door, grinning shyly as he ushered us into the room. Inside, the hut reeked of unventilated eons of sweating monks, dirty feet, and centuries of moldering candle wax and musky incense. A conical depression in the middle of the floor, at least a foot deep, spoke of untold centuries of monks shuffling their feet during morning prayers.

We took our place in the back, and a young, shaved-headed lad handed us prayer sticks. Immediately the monks launched into a soft, chanting meditation. I turned and asked Misgana, "Why do we need a prayer stick?"

He smiled. "Trust me, Mr. Bob; you'll need a prayer stick. These sessions can last a long time."

Joby and I tried to join in, but within minutes my calves and shins had begun to itch, then sting. I reached down to scratch and realized that fleas infested the hutch—and not just your typical American fleas but a feral African strain. My legs must have tasted like aged tenderloin compared to the monks' psoriasis-scarred limbs.

For the next three hours the carnivorous mites feasted inside my pant legs until I wanted to sprint from the hut, duck behind a tree, and strip down to my skivvies. But I didn't. After our rough introduction I didn't dare risk offending Abba by snubbing his prayer meeting. I had no feel for the island protocol, so I suffered in silence, praying for relief and for the vigil to end. Misgana told me later I could've exited at any moment without the slightest offense, but I had imagined my quiet torment as a sort of penance that might earn me access to the island's secrets.

Three hours later, as the sun began to rise over the lake, the monks finally broke for breakfast. I rushed into the sunlight and pulled up the cuff of my pants to see a leg sweaty and inflamed, sheathed in a crimson rash that would not subside until I returned to the States.[1] Raking the inside of my calves with my fingernails, I turned to Abba, and, as casually as I could, mentioned that I'd read Graham Hancock's book *The Sign and the Seal*. He nodded, unmoved; so I asked about the Hebrew pillars on the island's cliffs. He nodded again, this time mumbling a few words to Misgana.

Misgana leaned near and said, "Abba says he would be happy to show you."

I felt my pulse begin to race. I already knew the monks believed that when the ark left Jerusalem, it came first to Tana Kirkos. Only later—by some eight hundred years—did it make its way to Axum. Island tradition holds that Menelik's traveling party, searching for a safe haven for the precious relic, came to the eastern shore of Lake Tana in about 470 B.C. They had followed the Nile and its tributary, the Takazze, south from Egypt into Ethiopia, where the priests chose Tana Kirkos— even then regarded as a sacred lake, a holy place, dear to God[2]—for its high, fortresslike cliffs and rugged inaccessibility. There it remained, attended to by Jews, until approximately the fourth century (or about A.D. 330), when newly converted King Ezana made Christianity the country's official religion. Ezana then promptly sent for the ark and had it installed in a special chapel in Axum.[3]

This tradition differed from national legends only in the declaration that the ark landed first on Tana Kirkos. I knew that the monks here taught that the priests who brought the relic to Tana Kirkos maintained a strict Hebrew tradition of ritual cleansing and blood atonement sacrifices. And the purported existence of Hebrew pillars, located on a cliff above the village, seemed only to strengthen their case. I had come to see those pillars.

BLOOD OF THE ALTAR

Abba led us up a narrow path bordered by prickly, overgrown bushes to a series of rough stone steps emptying out onto a narrow plateau on the island's summit.

"This is where the ritual blood sacrifices took place centuries ago by the Jewish caretakers of the ark," Abba said, with Misgana translating.

Near the ledge stood a squat grouping of lichen-covered columns, hewn of granite and appearing not unlike heavily barnacled flotsam of ancient shipwrecks. The tallest column—conical shaped and square sided, standing perhaps five feet tall—had a cup-shaped, six-inch-deep depression carved out in its top. The other, shorter columns each had the same cup-shaped hollow.

The odd arrangement had no doubt been moved and reshuffled through the centuries yet still looked like an ancient altar. Abba demonstrated how the holes in each column had been used to collect blood during the ritual sacrifice of the lamb. Holding aloft an imaginary basin to illustrate how the ancient priests scattered blood over the stones, Abba pretended to pour the remaining blood into the hollows in the pillars. In both size and shape, the columns resembled the stone *masseboth* set up on high places in the earliest phases of Hebrew religion. These ritual altars served in sacrificial offering ceremonies much as Abba described.[4]

Abba showed us how the high priest dipped his right forefinger into a basin containing the blood, then scattered it over the stones and tent in an up-and-down, whiplike motion. He made a tipping movement, as if pouring blood from the imaginary basin into the cup-shaped hollows of the pillars. The manner in which he reenacted the sacrament seemed to mimic purification rites prescribed in Leviticus 4–5.

The columns did indeed seem appropriate to some bygone Hebrew ritual. But where did the *ark* fit in? Where did it sit beneath the tabernacle? I knew the monks had never revealed to any outsider precisely where the ark sat on the island. The best they could offer Graham Hancock was that it lay "somewhere near" the cliffs where we now stood.[5]

With nothing to lose, I decided to ask: "Abba, where did the ark sit?" My heart nearly skipped a beat when he casually pointed to the smooth granite beneath my feet.

"The ark sat right *here?*" Joby asked, looking down.

"Yes," Abba nodded.

Misgana chimed in: "He says the ark sat here, on this ledge, so that the blood could also be sprinkled on the tabernacle at the time of the sacrifice. This tradition has been passed down through the centuries."

I stared at the smooth surface of rock, perched high above the lagoon and surrounded on all sides by sheer cliffs. As a formidable watchtower from which to oppose seafaring invaders, the ledge made perfect sense. I bent down to inspect the granite surface, an unremarkable table of stone swathed in decaying leaves and layers of thatch.

I turned to Joby. "If the tabernacle sat *here*," I said, pausing, then thinking out loud. "If the tabernacle sat here, balanced on a solid slab of rock, how could a tent be secured on it? The winds whipping up this high would quickly blow any freestanding structure into the lagoon. Are there tent pegs, or socket holes for tent poles, somewhere about this ledge? If we could find evidence of a tabernacle on this plateau, it would lend weight to Abba's claim."

I got down on my knees and began poking around, pushing leaves and thatch aside and feeling for *something*—I wasn't sure what. I took out my knife and slid it down through the thick thatch, poking and prodding, sticking it into rocks and cracks, searching for a spot where the granite might yield to emptiness. Misgana, Joby, and Abba stared at me, clearly perplexed, but after a few minutes my knife found a hollow indentation in the rock.

"*Here!*" I said, quickly scooping out the dirt and leaves. "Joby, come help me."

Together we cleared the area. After some more digging, we managed to clean out a clearly defined socket hole, hidden beneath centuries of decayed organic matter, where a tent pole might have been anchored. It sat approximately twenty-five feet from the altar of pillars—by Abba's description, precisely where the tabernacle of the ark once stood.

I began clearing the rest of the ledge, probing the thatch and scree with my knife. After some minor excavation, I found a second hole, precisely where one might expect to find a second tent pole. Roughly the same circumference as the first, it lay in a south, east, west configuration from the other tent hole, covered by six inches of rotting palm fronds. While not as pronounced as the first, this one sat closer to the ledge and appeared to have been eroded by time.

93

I scoured the rest of the slab but never found the other two tent holes (if, indeed, that's what they had been). By the look of the ledge, the rock where the other holes would've been carved had been chipped and worn away by wind and erosion.

Next I noticed a small pile of rocks stacked next to the altar—a makeshift shrine? Among the chunks sat a sizable piece of granite with a tent-pole-sized hole carved in the top. By appearances alone it might have been a third socket hole, long since broken away from the ledge. Who knew? Abba didn't, and after a few more minutes spent scraping in the leaves, I told Joby, "I think we've found all we're going to find up here."

As we walked back down the trail, my mind swirled with provocative scenarios: Had we just stood on the *Shetiyyah* of Tana Kirkos, the foundation stone of an ancient Ethiopian Holy of Holies? Had I hollowed out the contours of the tent holes that once supported the tabernacle of the ark? Were Joby and I the first westerners to learn of the ark's location on the cliffs? I noticed Abba eyeing me with some interest, his expression registering an uneasy tension at the discovery of the tent-peg holes, as if he had never seen them.

Minutes later, Misgana confirmed it. "I don't think they knew the holes were there," he whispered.

It didn't surprise me. The ledge clearly hadn't been maintained, and the tent holes probably seemed a matter of minor consequence to the ancient monks after the ark departed. Since the relic no longer rested here, it didn't require much imagination to see how time could obscure such evidence.

"Joby," I said, "if those holes signify what I think they do, then both of us stood precisely where the holy ark once sat. We stood where the tent (or tabernacle) and the Holy of Holies would've been."

MYSTERIOUS ARTIFACTS

Back at the village, Abba disappeared for a moment into a locked hut while Joby and I waited outside. Misgana explained, "I believe the elder has something else to show you."

Emerging a few minutes later, Abba placed a small mat on the ground on which we could sit. He laid another mat a few feet in front of us. Then he instructed a helper to help him. From the hut they carried a large basin. Broad and shallow—approximately two feet wide, though no more than a couple of inches deep—the basin had become so pitted and oxidized with a green patina that I couldn't easily identify the metal. Because of what Abba said next, however, I guessed it was bronze.

"The ancient Hebrews who brought the ark to Lake Tana called it a *gomer*," he explained. "They used it up on the cliffs to collect the blood used in the ritual sacrifices."

Though I'd never heard the word *gomer* (even Abba didn't know its origin), I suspected it had to be the Hebrew basin he had described earlier at the stone monoliths. Abba reentered the storage hut and returned, balancing a heavy, bulky tangle of metal in both hands. Consisting of single, cast-iron rods fused about a circular lip at both top and bottom, it had once been a sturdy bronze stand, he said, long since collapsed. Abba didn't seem to know its exact purpose, but its mottled edges, encrusted with the same bluish pits and white corrosion as the basin, had a deep, red-brown color. The opening at the top seemed to be about the same dimensions as the bronze basin.

Cradling the basin like a newborn baby, Abba again described how it had been used to scatter blood in Jewish sacrifices. Yet the more I looked, the more the basin and stand seemed to reflect passages in Exodus and Leviticus describing "basin and stand" as an integrated unit for ritual cleansing (Exod. 30:17–19). Or the passage regarding the sacred anointing oil used to consecrate "the Tent of Meeting" (Exod. 30:26–29). Both basin and stand also appear in Leviticus, when Moses ordained Aaron and his sons for the priesthood (Lev. 8:10–11).

While Abba and his predecessors interpreted the basin as an instrument for blood sacrifice, I assumed the passage of time had perhaps muddled the traditions. I suspected that the basin and stand had once been components for ritual washing.

It didn't really matter. These implements possibly shared a Hebrew origin, and the monks on Tana Kirkos had neither the resources nor technology to forge metal. Someone obviously brought them here. I thought of the silver trumpets at the Axum chapel and wondered: *Could this basin and stand have been among the original temple vessels, forged in Moses' time and placed in Solomon's temple for service before the ark? Had these instruments actually come to Tana Kirkos with the ark?*

"Mr. Bob!" Misgana whispered, nudging me. Abba had just then reemerged from the hut holding a long, two-pronged instrument that looked like a giant tuning fork. I quickly identified it as consistent with yet another Hebrew sacrificial implement—a meat fork used to burn sacrifices over ritual fires.

"Abba says it is a meat fork," Misgana agreed, "left on the island by those who brought the ark!"

Heavily rusted and showing signs of wear similar to the stand and basin, the implement's long, double prongs met at a horizontal bridge at the top, crowned by what I took to be an old Axumite cross. Abba clarified: "It is not a cross, but the image of a budding almond flower."

An almond flower? My mind drifted back to Jabal al Lawz in Saudi Arabia. That black-crowned peak, now recognized by many as the real Mount Sinai (see my book, *In Search of the Mountain of God*), once served as the likely construction site of the ark of the covenant. Its English translation means "mountain of the almond flower."

Throughout the Old Testament the budding almond ranked high in Israel's sacred iconography, adorning many vessels used in the Tent of Meeting and in the first temple (Exod. 25:33–34; 37:19–20). Who can forget the story of Aaron's staff, budding overnight with an almond flower (Num. 17:8)? That same staff, regarded as the tool of one of Yahweh's great Old Testament miracles, ultimately lay alongside the holy manna and Ten Commandments within the ark of the covenant (Heb. 9:4). Certainly, as Scripture makes clear, ritual meat forks played prominently in the altar of burnt offering (Exod. 27:3; 38:3; Num. 4:14; 2 Chron. 4:16).

Meat forks, bronze basins, bronze stands! So far as I knew, no westerner had ever seen these items. Had they indeed once served in the temple of Solomon? If we had seen only one or two of these ancient artifacts, I might have written it off as a strange coincidence. Yet taken together—the cliff shrine, the pillars for blood sacrifice, the hidden tent holes, and now the basin, stand, and meat fork—we seemed to have uncovered interlocking pieces of a fantastic puzzle. Each of these vessels and components appeared much like those described in Scripture; each made an arguable case for Tana Kirkos as an ancient Hebrew haven; and each seemed to suggest a resting place for the ark of the covenant.

I turned to Abba: "Would you allow me to scrape off a bit of metal from the gomer or the meat forks, to take it back to the States to test for their age?" I knew his answer before I asked (but I *had* to ask). Abba frowned and shook his head.

"No, Mr. Bob," Misgana said, "under no circumstances can you do such a thing. These are sacred vessels."

I stood up and took a deep breath, glancing skyward to see an enormous, white-tailed eagle gliding over the cliffs.

"Joby, let's get our things together. It's time to go."

Sunlight had faded into dusk. It had been a full, profitable day, and our pilot didn't like to be out on the water much past dark. I could now leave, satisfied that I'd learned, seen, even touched much more than expected.

I knew I would return one day, soon. Other evidence must be scattered about the island. We bid a fond, slow farewell to Abba and the other monks and donated a tidy sum to their village—to buy what, I couldn't begin to guess. Hauling our bags and equipment down the trail to the lagoon, we turned to see a small, frail-looking monk shuffling after us with some urgency.

I didn't recognize him at first, but then realized his identity—"Joby, this is the fellow with the infection you treated."

Joby did a double take, then yelped, "He's *walking!*"

Indeed, the fellow's face beamed. And he walked, straight up, for the first time in weeks. As he approached, he extended his hands, and in his thin, calloused fingers we saw three shriveled limes.

"It is an offering of thanks," Misgana said. "It is all he has."

Realizing that this old monk wanted to give us what likely constituted his life's possessions, Joby and I reluctantly accepted the gift. We bowed toward one another, exchanging grateful smiles. Then, with tears in his eyes, the old monk began thanking us with extravagant smiles and gestures of gratitude.

"He is in your debt and asks you to take the limes as a blessing," Misgana said, adding, "He didn't think he'd ever walk again."

I carefully placed the limes in my bag and said good-bye. We loaded our gear on the skiff and helped the pilot push off. I turned to see Abba walking down the trail. He stood on the rocks, smiling and waving good-bye.

"You have made new friends, Mr. Bob," Misgana quipped, hopping down from the bow. He tossed his tiny pack in the cabin and then added, "Abba told me they would welcome you back, anytime."

More than all the treasures that this journey had yielded, those few words from a Tana Kirkos holy man made the trip for me. With the sun now lying low over Lake Tana, we turned into the waves and sailed south across the expanse. The trip had been a roaring success, but I was eager to return home. My first visit to Ethiopia had come and gone, and now I felt far better equipped to face the challenges ahead.

✝ E Π

TOO PROVOCATIVE TO DISMISS

After I returned home to Colorado, I weighed the prospects of probing deeper into the mystery of the ark in Ethiopia and found the possibilities too provocative to dismiss. I had little proof but vivid impressions of what might lay inside the chapel at Axum.

Now I desired to let the world see these sights through my eyes; I sought to produce a video, perhaps even a book, on the subject. If I'd seen enough in an initial visit to incite my imagination, what might I find if I actually spent some real time in Ethiopia? So many questions remained; so much had yet to be learned and discovered.

NEW LEADS, NEW APPROACHES

While Ethiopia entered the twenty-first century cloaked in mystery, it made no effort to hide its tradition regarding the last resting place of the most holy object in history. As one theory among many, it deserved to be taken seriously, if for no other reason than the relic hadn't turned up anywhere else.

I traveled to Ethiopia several times in the next few years, furthering my research and pursuing the friendships I'd made along the way. In so doing, my comfort level with the idea of the ark in Axum kept growing, confronting me with questions: What does a sacred object, so widely revered yet so rarely seen, look like? Does it match the biblical description of the ark? Are there living eyewitnesses who have actually *seen* it? Why had it ended up in Axum?

My faith in the sovereignty of God told me that, if indeed the ark had made its way to Ethiopia, then God must have had a good reason for sending it there. New leads kept popping up, paving fresh avenues for research.

In the same period I also traveled to Jerusalem to interview Falasha Jews who resettled there during a 1984 airlift known as Operation Moses. In addition to meeting the Falashas, the visit gave me an opportunity to scout the city's relevant biblical sites: the Temple Mount, the Dome of the Rock, other first temple landmarks. I also wanted to interview Hebrew scholars versed in ancient Judaism's missing ark theories.

At Jerusalem's Hebrew Institute, for example, I interviewed social anthropologist Dr. Shalva Weil, who described the Ethiopian Jews as modern-day descendants of Old Testament Hebrews who traveled to Egypt centuries ago. After settling in Egypt for a time, she said, they made their way south through Nubia (southern Egypt and northern Sudan) eventually to occupy northern Ethiopia. When I asked about the possibility of the ark of the covenant resting at the chapel at Axum, she grinned, drew a deep breath, and admitted, "There is a strong connection that the Ethiopian Christians possess the ark."

From Israel I flew to Egypt to visit Elephantine Island, where archaeologists had unearthed evidence of an ancient Hebrew temple from King Manasseh's time. Archaeologists concluded that the island might have served as a stopping off point for the ark en route to Ethiopia.

These side trips afforded me a visual connection to prominent places and events and helped me fill in some chronological gaps in the ark narrative. In Jerusalem, for example, I interviewed a Falasha priest who confirmed the Tana Kirkos' tradition, that, after being removed from the first temple, the ark languished for two hundred years in Egypt before continuing its southward trek to Tana Kirkos Island. Eight hundred years later (and nearly two thousand years removed from its flight from Jerusalem), the ark left Tana Kirkos and traveled to Axum, transplanted by King Ezana, where it remains to this day. It felt useful to have an Ethiopian *Hebrew* confirming events to which the Christian monks on Tana Kirkos had so confidently attested.

ELEPHANTINE ISLAND

On Elephantine Island I filmed and interviewed Egyptian archaeologists who told me of the existence of papyrus scrolls and potsherds (written by Hebrews in Aswan to those in Jerusalem in the mid-seventh century)[1] with references to a "temple of Yahweh" used to shelter none other than the "Person of God." Hebrews had built the replica temple about 650 B.C., during the reign of Judah's King Manasseh. Hostile Egyptians destroyed it some two hundred years later, in approximately 410 B.C.

Although some scholars believe the community on Elephantine consisted of Hebrew mercenaries, others surmise it included a mix of refugees, including Levitical priests seeking sanctuary from wicked King Manasseh's persecution.[2]

Could this Elephantine temple, modeled after the first temple and located on the east bank of the Nile, have served as a temporary resting place for the ark? Though such a temple on Egyptian soil would have constituted a serious violation of Israelite law, which forbade the construction of any temple or conducting ritual sacrifices outside of Jerusalem (Ps. 132:13–14; Ezra 6:12), it may have been rationalized in the face of Manasseh's excesses. In any event the Elephantine Hebrews clearly thought that Yahweh resided physically in their temple (a number of papyri speak of Yahweh as "dwelling" there).[3] And if such a temple were built to house the ark, it helps explain why, if the ark disappeared from Jerusalem in the early to mid 600s B.C., the relic didn't arrive in Ethiopia until approximately 470 B.C.

Had the Levites, in fact, taken the ark to Elephantine Island in approximately 680 B.C., placing it in a replica temple built especially to house it? And when Egyptian goodwill crumbled two hundred years later, did they then proceed south into Ethiopia, installing the ark on Tana Kirkos? Is Elephantine Island a missing link between Jerusalem and Ethiopia?

Trying to answer these questions kept me returning to Ethiopia, looking for new clues and hints, gaining insight into obscure creeds, and plugging holes in the scholarly record. Taken together, a mounting trail of evidence kept me hopeful that, if the ark still existed, it likely rested in Axum's simple chapel.

DID THE ARK TRAVEL TO EGYPT?

Does the Bible say that the ark traveled to Egypt? No, but many clues suggest that it may have.

Most commentators believe that Scripture gives no clues as to the fate of the ark, but I wonder about that. Among the many theories regarding the time and circumstances of the ark's disappearance, one of the most startling suggests that young King Josiah tried to reclaim the holy relic.

When Manasseh defiled the temple and raised up pagan idols all over Israel, he provoked God into declaring that he would destroy Jerusalem and the temple, then send his people into exile (2 Kings 23:26–27; Jer. 15). That prophecy would finally come true fifty-six years later—yet not until an amazing series of events had unfolded.

Following Manasseh came the brief, two-year reign of Amon, who walked in his father's wicked footsteps. Ultimately he was assassinated. His untimely death set the stage for Amon's son, Josiah, to become king at the tender age of eight.

When Josiah was eighteen years old, Scripture tells us "the Book of the Law of the LORD given by Moses" (2 Chron. 34:14 NKJV) was discovered in a part of the temple complex where it had lain hidden from Manasseh. Josiah reacted to the reading of God's Word by tearing his robes in grief. Immediately he cleansed Israel of idols and restored national worship of the one true God. A powerful revival broke out, with the temple soon repaired and the priesthood revived.

103
∧

The zealousness of the king astonished observers; perhaps Josiah's zeal led him to think that God might relent from destroying Jerusalem. To learn whether this might be so, the king inquired of God's prophetess, Huldah, and learned that because of Manasseh's wickedness, Israel and the temple would indeed be destroyed (2 Kings 22:17–20). Yet in God's mercy Josiah would die before these terrible things occurred (v. 20).

Josiah must have felt crushed. After all, he had cleansed the temple and rid the nation of its mediums, spiritists, and detestable idols. Was there nothing he could do to stay God's hand? Would Jerusalem and the temple really be destroyed and the people sent into exile?

Despite a heavy heart, Josiah continued his reforms, renewed the covenant of the book of the law, and reinstituted the biblical feasts, including a memorable Passover celebration. During this unprecedented Passover—the likes of which had not been seen since the days of the judges (2 Chron. 35:18)—Josiah issued a public plea that still shocks us today. He ordered the Levites to "put the holy ark in the house which Solomon the son of David, king of Israel, built." Then he told the priests that the ark "shall no longer be a burden on your shoulders."

And in a final admonishment, he urged them, "Now serve the LORD your God and His people Israel" (2 Chron. 35:3 NKJV).

From this short passage, nearly lost in the long record of Josiah's reforms, we can discern at least four major clues as to its whereabouts:

1. The ark was definitely *not* in the Jerusalem temple at this point in Josiah's reign. But if the ark wasn't in Jerusalem, when had it departed, and why?
2. Wherever it had gone, the ark apparently had been transported in correct fashion: on the shoulders of the Levites, by means of poles (see 1 Chron. 15:15). The passage implies that the ark had been employed in tabernacle worship—entirely possible since the tabernacle had long been in storage in or near the temple (1 Kings 8:4).
3. The ark remained in the possession of true Levites of Israel.
4. Josiah bluntly challenged the Levites to "serve the LORD your God and His people Israel."

This last item bears closer scrutiny, as it seems to reveal Josiah's strained attitude toward the Levites. If they truly had the ark in their possession, then Josiah's exhortation suggests that they had, in some sense, ceased serving the Lord and the people of Israel. But if the Levites were indeed correctly transporting the ark and using it in tabernacle worship, then what people—if not the Israelites—were they serving?

It is interesting to note that Josiah's reign (early to mid 600s B.C.) closely corresponds to the construction of the Hebrew temple on Egypt's Elephantine Island. If, as we believe, the Levites fled with the ark to Egypt during Manasseh's reign, then Josiah's charge may have resounding implications: he may have been commanding the Levites to stop serving the *Egyptians* and return the ark to the temple in Jerusalem!

Of one thing we can be sure: the ark did not reside in Solomon's temple during Josiah's reign. And were it not for what happens next in the biblical record, we might let the matter rest. But Josiah does something utterly mystifying.

After successfully instituting reforms that turned Israel's heart back to God (however briefly), the young king committed a deed altogether rash. Second Chronicles 35:20 tells us the final act of Josiah's rule: "After all this, when Josiah had set the temple in order, . . . Josiah marched out to meet [Neco, king of Egypt] in battle." The passage raises at least two troubling questions:

1. What does Scripture mean that Josiah "set the temple in order"?
2. What prompted this godly king to wage an unwise battle against Pharaoh Neco?

To address the first question, let's interrupt the narrative to examine the various ways the phrase, "set the temple in order," has been translated into English.

> "After all this, when Josiah had set the temple in order" (NIV).
> "After all this, when Josiah had set the temple in order" (NASB).
> "After all this, when Josiah had prepared the temple" (KJV).
> "After all this, when Josiah had prepared the temple" (NKJV).

What Josiah accomplished in the temple just prior to his death sheds light on whether the ark had indeed returned to Jerusalem during his reign. The first translations, "set the temple in order," imply that Josiah's call to return the ark to the temple had been heeded. Such a translation suggests that the Levites had obeyed his command and that the ark had been restored to its rightful place in the Holy of Holies.

Yet appearances can be deceiving. The original Hebrew phrase consists of a one-word compound (*hekin*) derived from a root word (*kun*), which has a range of meanings centered on the concepts "prepare," "establish," and "make ready"—*not* "set in order." The precise form of *hekin* used in 2 Chronicles 35:20 can also be found in nineteen other passages, in all but one meaning simply "prepared."

Therefore, rather than indicating that everything in the temple had been "set in order," the passage implies that Josiah "prepared" the temple, in the same way that one prepares one's heart. Since Josiah already had cleansed the temple and eradicated from it all traces of idolatry, 2 Chronicles 35:20 must mean that Josiah "prepared" the temple to receive the one item that could make it—and Israel—whole again: the ark and the mercy seat. The passage gives us a portrait of an expectant Israel poised to reclaim its lost glory.

Poised, yes, but with one fatal flaw—regardless of Josiah's righteous intent, any attempt to return the ark and the mercy seat to the temple would directly contradict what God had revealed about Israel's destruction. Despite Josiah's house-cleaning campaign, God still declared, "I will reject Jerusalem, the city I chose, and this temple, about which I said, 'There shall my Name be'" (2 Kings 23:27). By God's decree, the ark would not come back into the temple.

So where did this leave Josiah? Of a mind, perhaps, to take matters into his own hands?

After Josiah prepared the temple to receive the ark, he led his army out to fight Pharaoh Neco, who was on his way to fight the Babylonians (2 Chron. 35:20). Why would Josiah pick a fight with Pharaoh immediately after preparing the temple for the return of the ark? The text doesn't say, except to inform us that Neco sent messengers warning Josiah to stay away: "What have I to do with you, king of Judah? I have not come against you this day, but against the house with which I have war" (v. 21 NKJV). Then, in a most telling statement, Neco adds, "for God commanded me to make haste." A closer

↑ 1. Rising to importance about the time of the birth of Christ, the town of Axum was once the capital of the far-reaching Axumite Kingdom. Its distant regal past revolves around a strong tradition that Ethiopian King Ezana brought the original ark of the covenant to Axum in about A.D. 331, after the country converted to Christianity and captured the ark from Ethiopian Jews.

↑ 2. The Chapel of St. Mary of Zion, known as the mother church of Ethiopian Orthodoxy, was built in 1964 on orders of then-Emperor Haile Selassie. Ethiopians believe that within the dark recesses of this solemn compound lies one of the most sacred relics of history—the original ark of the covenant.

← 3. The object within the Chapel of St. Mary of Zion is attended to by a succession of lone guardians, or *atangs*, until their death, when a new guardian is chosen. Here a young monk-in-training, sequestered within the monastery compound throughout childhood, visits a friend through an iron fence.

↓ 4. Bob and Paul Cornuke inspect Axum's famous stelae park. The massive obelisks, carved from single pieces of granite, serve as monuments to bygone kings. Some Axumite traditions claim the powers of the ark of the covenant had been used to raise the towering monoliths.

↑ 5. Axum lays claim to the biblical queen of Sheba, who, according to ancient Ethiopian tradition, conceived a son with Israel's King Solomon — Prince Menelik I — who Ethiopians believe returned to Jerusalem as a young man and stole the ark. Here, a huge water reservoir in Axum, known as the Queen of Sheba's Bath, forms the focal point of the annual Timkat (Epiphany) ceremony.

← 6. The co-author examining an engraving on a fallen stela in Axum. The engraving is believed to represent the ark of the covenant.

← 7. Cornuke explores Axum's underground galleries and chambers, this one used as a treasury by Emperor Kaleb (A.D. 514–542). Additional tunnels and rooms, still under excavation, extend far into the surrounding hillsides and are thought by some to offer escape routes for the ark should Axum ever come under attack.

↑ 8.-8a.-8b. — Axum's annual Timkat ceremony, January 18–19, gives locals a chance to celebrate Ethiopia's rich ark tradition. Throughout the two-day event, Christian priests carry ornate replicas of the ark, or *tabots*, through the streets on their heads, while revelers chant and cheer and play musical instruments like those used in religious ceremonies in Israel during Old Testament times. The pageant symbolizes the biblical dance of David before the ark. →

← 9. Mornings in Axum cast the city in an ancient, eery light, as white-robed Christians congregate about the Chapel of St. Mary of Zion, praying, worshiping, and reading their red-bound *Ge'ez* Bibles amid stone fortifications several hundred years old.

↓ 10. Ancient frescoes of angelic beings, like these found on walls and ceilings of churches throughout northern Ethiopia, are thought to represent the cherubim described in Scripture, overshadowing the mercy seat of the ark of the covenant (Exod. 25:18).

11.–11a.. — A monk at the Chapel of St. Mary of Zion displays an archaic silver trumpet, wrapped tightly for protection and purported to have been taken from Solomon's temple at the same time as the ark of the covenant. The size and design of the trumpets indeed seem to match the image of Hebrew trumpets carved into the Arch of Titus in Rome (11a), erected following the sacking of Jerusalem and the destruction of the Second Temple by Titus in A.D. 70.↑

← 13. Axum guide Birani Miscal (left), holding a wooden Axumite cross, introduced the co-author to a former monk (right) within the St. Mary of Zion Monastery. The monk said he had glimpsed the actual ark of the covenant on several occasions in the course of his duties.

↑ 12. BASE board member Ray Ardizonne posing with Axum children during a junket to Ethiopia.

← 14. On their final visit to Axum, the co-authors met this elderly monk, who claimed to have ventured, with two others, into the forbidden inner sanctum of the chapel of the ark. "My body feels like it is dying," he said, describing the effects of gazing upon the object believed to be the original ark and mercy seat.

15.–15a.–15b The new Jerusalem: the eleven stone churches of Lalibella are spectacular monolithic structures hewn from solid volcanic rock in the twelfth century after Christ. The architect, Ethiopian Prince Lalibella, spent twenty-five years in exile in Jerusalem and, some believe, returned to build the churches as a sacred repository for the ark of the covenant. Today a sect of Christian priests (15b) spend their days praying and worshiping within the labyrinth of stone caves, chiseled paths, and galleries tucked amid the churches.

← 16. A Knight Templar cross inside a star of David, carved into columns and ceilings of certain Lalibella churches, support theories that the Knights Templars helped build the magnificent churches as a means of gaining favor with the Ethiopian rulers, possibly in hopes of someday capturing the ark.

↓ 17. Remnants of war can be seen throughout northern Ethiopia. In Gondar, home to some of Ethiopia's most celebrated castles and churches, it is common to find gutted, bullet-riddled husks of military transport vehicles littering the streets.

← 18. Traditional Ethiopian coffee ceremony. In the Falasha Jewish village of Weleka outside Gondar, a humble Ethiopian Jew named Marye offers warmth and hospitality to her American visitors.

↓ 20. Two women from unfamiliar worlds. Mary Irwin, wife of astronaut Jim Irwin, formed a quick bond with Marye of Weleka, who came to regard her Christian guests with familial affection.

19. Coauthors David Halbrook (left) and Bob Cornuke interview Marye about her people's ancient ark traditions. Though most of the Falashas have since been airlifted to Israel, leaving only a few women and children behind, the presence in modern Ethiopia of black Jews, nearly two thousand miles from Israel, strikes ark enthusiasts as something more than an odd curiosity. ↓

← 21. The hollowed, hammered gold molding of King Tut's mask provides clues to the size, weight, and configuration of the cherubim overshadowing the ark and mercy seat.

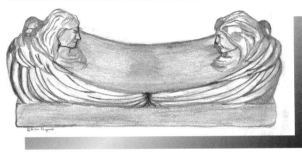

↙ 22. (Photo of Parker Fitzgerald's artistic rendering of the cherubim and mercy seat.) "And you shall make two cherubim of gold; of hammered work you shall make them at the two ends of the mercy seat" (Exod. 25:18 NKJV). Like Pharaoh's mask, the wings of the cherubim atop the atonement cover of the ark were made of pure, hammered gold, giving them a solid appearance without the mass of a large, cast image. This technique tells us the natural posture of the wings probably would be to blanket the mercy seat like a quilt, flowing down in a U-shaped arc, accommodating its functional use as a literal throne for the returning king.

↑ 23. "A nation powerful and treading down, whose land the rivers divide" (Isa. 18:7 NJKV). Majestic Blue Nile Falls, just south of Lake Tana, feeds into the Blue Nile, which rambles north, carrying life and fertility through Sudan to Egypt's Nile Delta. The fertile Ethiopian plateau, crisscrossed by rivers and streams, conjures a verse from Zephaniah 3:10: "From beyond the rivers of Cush my worshipers, my scattered people, will bring me offerings."

← 24. Dawn crests on massive Lake Tana, whose many secluded islands, some believe, may have once sheltered the ark of the covenant. Might this land of raging rivers and swollen lakes one day render back to its rightful homeland the ultimate offering—the gift of the holy ark?

↑ 25. The imposing cliffs of Tana Kirkos Island, rising high above the waves of Lake Tana, once may have sheltered the ark of the covenant. Its remote location and difficult access would have provided a formidable fortress for an ancient sect of Levite priests believed by locals to have guarded the holy relic for eight hundred years.

↑ 26.–26a. On a narrow plateau on the summit of Tana Kirkos sit lichen-covered stone columns, hewn of granite, with holes carved out (26b) for collecting blood used in animal sacrifices. Island tradition holds that Ethiopian Prince Menelik's caravan, searching for a safe haven for the ark, came to the eastern shore of Lake Tana in 470 B.C., and that Levite priests maintained a strict Hebrew regimen of ritual cleansing and blood sacrifice.

↑ 27. On the same narrow ledge, claim local Christian monks, the ark of the covenant sat sheltered for eight hundred years beneath a Jewish-style tabernacle. Under a moldering pile of loose leaves and thatch, Cornuke found holes he believed could have been socket holes for tent poles.

↑ 28.–28a. After spending time in the monks' village, Cornuke was surprised to be shown ancient temple vessels said to have been brought to the island along with the ark from Solomon's Temple. Among these were aged and rusted meat forks thought to be used in burnt offerings; a bronze basin (the locals call it a *gomer*) likely used in ritual cleansing (Exod. 30:17–19); and a basin stand, twisted and bent from age and fatigue. Standing next to Cornuke (28) is Abba Baye, the chief priest of the Christian monastery on Tana Kirkos.

↑ 29. The coauthors standing with Abba Baye, holding an ancient meat fork, crowned with the forged image of an almond flower. In the Book of Numbers, Aaron's staff miraculously budded overnight into an almond flower, and was ultimately placed within the ark of the covenant (Num. 17:8; Exod. 25:33–34; Heb. 9:4).

↑ 30. Ancient, goatskin manuscripts stored on Tana Kirkos depict the boy Jesus together with Mary, sailing to Tana Kirkos to visit the ark.

↑ 31.–31a. Mary Irwin, wife of astronaut Jim Irwin, presents Ethiopian President Negaso Gidada a framed Ethiopian tricolor flag (31a) that had once traveled with her husband to the moon. Also pictured are Bob Cornuke, BASE board member Pete Leininger, and his wife Barbara. →

↑ 32. The co-authors introduce President Gidada to their theory from Isaiah 18, of a great gift, or "offering," coming out of Ethiopia, or Cush, at the time of Messiah's victorious return. The theory states that the ark of the covenant with the top of the ark, known as the mercy seat or atonement cover, is the offering that will be brought out of Ethiopia to serve as the literal throne of Christ in the Messianic Temple.

↑ 33. The BASE Institute traveling party posed with Ethiopia's president and high officials outside the Ethiopian National Palace.

Photos by Daniel Ayres, David Halbrook, and Bob Cornuke.

look reveals that, in this instance at least, the king of Egypt was taking orders directly from the God of Israel.

Neco scolds Josiah, saying, "Refrain from meddling with God, who is with me, lest He destroy you" (v. 21 NKJV). In Hebrew the statement doesn't mean merely, "God is on my side." Rather, the preposition can indicate that God was actually *with* Neco, literally in his company. In a dramatic statement that goes almost unnoticed, Neco informs Josiah that the God of the Hebrews was with him, personally, on-site! This amazing bit of dialogue reveals two crucial points:

1. Neco had received his orders directly from God himself.
2. God was literally with him in the camp of Egypt.

In times past both of these statements had been made of Israel—but only when the ark traveled with the nation. With the ark in front of Israel's armies, God had led his people into battle, speaking to them from between the cherubim. Could Neco here be making a claim that could be true only if he actually possessed the ark and the mercy seat? Was God actually *with* Neco, relaying orders from the ark? The best standard to judge might be found in the reliability of Neco's warning to Josiah.

Not only did Neco's army rout Israel, but Josiah himself died in the ill-advised battle. Verse 22 states: "Nevertheless Josiah would not turn his face from [Neco], but disguised himself so that he might fight with him" (NKJV). Josiah had refused to heed Neco's warning and even went so far as to disguise himself. Did he think that he could hide from God? Could it be that Josiah simply could not bear the thought that Israel's crown jewel, the ark, remained in Pharaoh's hands—especially after going to such lengths to prepare the temple?

Whatever the truth, we have this statement—from the author of 2 Chronicles, not from the lips of Neco—hinting that Pharaoh may indeed have possessed the ark and the mercy seat. The scribe of 2 Chronicles boldly asserts that Josiah "did not heed the words of Necho *from the mouth of God*"—an incredible phrase, confirming that Neco's warning had come from the sovereign Lord himself. It appears as though Neco had not been merely posturing or saber rattling; he told the truth!

According to the Bible, Neco received his instructions directly from the "mouth of God"—a phrase which points intriguingly toward the ark. Scripture says that the voice of God (indicating God's manifest presence) came from above the mercy seat, from between the cherubim (Num. 7:89). If, then, Scripture tells us that Neco received his information directly from the mouth of God, may we not envision God speaking from his place above the mercy seat, between the cherubim?

Is it possible that this tragic event in Josiah's otherwise exemplary life provides a clue to an age-old riddle, alerting us that the ark had indeed been taken into Egypt by priests fleeing the atrocities of Manasseh? Might it also tell us that, during Josiah's reign, the ark and the mercy seat sometimes traveled with the army of Neco, king of Egypt? Could it also be that Josiah's purpose in confronting Neco had been to take back the ark by force, even though God had made clear that Jerusalem and the temple would be destroyed?

If so, it meant that Josiah's act not only fulfilled Huldah's prophecy about his death. (Josiah perished before God's punishment came upon Israel.) It also could mean that the ark remained safely with the Egyptians rather than being taken as plunder when Nebuchadnezzar sacked Jerusalem thirteen years later.

Could such an astonishing scenario really have happened? If the ark had indeed been spirited out of Jerusalem during Manasseh's reign of terror, it seems not at all unlikely that it would stop first in Egypt, perhaps even on the island of Elephantine. Josiah, in all good conscience, may well have tried and failed to recapture the ark. His sad story may well add to a cryptic body of evidence pointing toward the resting place of the ark . . . in Ethiopia.

Eleven

MISSION IMPOSSIBLE

I had two goals in mind for my second trip to Axum in the winter of 1998. First, I wanted to continue my research and videotape my findings. Second, I planned to bring in medicine and some stopgap health care to the Ethiopians.

I never imagined I'd get to meet the guardian of the ark.

DISEASE IN AXUM

Upon reaching Addis Ababa, I led the team—my son, Brandon, then a senior in high school; retired Colorado Springs doctor, Dr. Jim Gaba, and his wife, Paula; Jim Fitzgerald; Steve Griesen; and two videographers, David Stotts and Brian Boorujy—on a quick tour of the city. We also left medicine and supplies at a dirt-poor, ill-equipped orphanage in the inner city slums.

The next morning we caught a flight to Axum, where I hooked up once again with my wise, old friend, Birani Misqaul. He seemed happy to see me and promptly arranged for us to pay a visit to the monks of St. Mary of Zion. There in a darkened church annex we prayed together and treated sufferers for everything from eye infections to stomach ailments and chronic arthritis.

On this visit the monks seemed eager for Dr. Gaba to check their pulses, flash his light in their eyes, and prescribe antacids and antibiotics. That morning we moved our offices to the center of town and set up a makeshift clinic on a card table inside a dirt-floored, doorless shack. Here, in the crudest surroundings, Dr. Gaba—who'd traveled all over the world on missionary tours—calmly slipped on his white frock and hung a stethoscope around his neck. With Brandon by his side, he set up his doctor's kit and began stacking boxes of medicine behind the table.

"Shouldn't we put up a sign or something?" Brandon asked, curious as to how the sick and needy might find them.

"Get ready, here they come," Dr. Gaba calmly answered.

Within minutes hundreds of ailing Axumites, drawn as if by radar, converged on the shack. Minutes later the line, five people abreast, trailed down the street and around the block. The crush pinned Brandon and Dr. Gaba to the back of the shanty, and in the chaos they found it impossible to tend to the most serious cases. Everyone, it seemed, suffered to some degree from malnutrition.

Dr. Gaba worked feverishly, squirting countless vials of eye ointment into eyes ravaged by microscopic fly larvae, administering injections and antibiotics, and managing to treat dozens before the throng swelled to a dangerous size. In the end, with the shanty's walls about to burst, Dr. Gaba and Brandon had no choice but to fold up shop and push their way out of the shack.

Brandon arrived back at the hotel, stunned by what he had just seen, his heart broken by the futility of their efforts. His mind could not grasp the sight of so many crippled and infirm.

"We couldn't help them all," he said, his voice choking back emotion. "We couldn't even *begin* to help them."

He'd just witnessed what I had seen on my first trip. Despite our noblest efforts, our small team didn't stand a chance. The sad truth? Instead of five boxes of supplies, we could've brought in five truckloads of medicine and mobilized several teams of doctors, and still we wouldn't have made a dent. One little boy kept begging Brandon, with outstretched arms, to help his emaciated, two-year-old brother, lying sick in the dust and probably dying.

"Looking at that little boy took away my breath," he told me that night. "I wanted so badly to do something, to whisk him to the front of the line; but I realized it would mean that someone else wouldn't get help." The line had flooded over with mothers and grandmothers holding out sick babies and children, something Dr. Gaba had seen countless times. Touched by Brandon's youthful anguish, he tried to explain, with a frankness borne of his own oft-crushed illusions, that terrible suffering remains a common theme around the globe.

"Brandon," he said gently, "you have just experienced a typical day in the Third World. The size of the problems defies our puny imaginations. You do your best in these situations, do what you can."

What Brandon saw and felt on that trip radically altered his worldview. He'd brought $180 with him for spending money, but from the time we landed to the moment we boarded our plane for the States, he gave it all away. On the last night of our trip, after we had dropped off our last medical supplies at the dirty and dilapidated orphanage in Addis, Brandon turned around, walked over to a small, black-robed nurse, turned his wallet upside down and gave her the last of his money. "After seeing what I've seen," he said to me, "how can I leave this country with a single penny?"

I put my arm around him and smiled. It made me proud to see his heart breaking for these people of whom I'd become so fond.

"Brandon," I said, "you may be young in the world's eyes, but tonight you became a man."

THE GUARDIAN

Early the next morning, Birani appeared at our hotel door, all black robes and gray hair and shriveled hands. Bowing, he asked me quietly, "Would you like to meet with the guardian today?"

I rubbed my eyes. "Did I hear you right, Birani?"

I hadn't mentioned the guardian, but Birani knew from the last trip of my hopes. He had made the arrangements, unsolicited. Of course, I eagerly accepted.

After breakfast we followed Birani down the hill to the rear gate of the sanctuary of St. Mary of Zion. After waiting several minutes at the spiked iron fence—where the chapel curator had earlier shown us the royal crowns and trumpets—the guardian strolled down the back steps and met our team, greeting us all warmly.

Abba Mekonen, age sixty-nine, known as Atang, or the "keeper of the ark," struck me as a typically bone-thin, handsome Ethiopian, wearing only slightly more elaborate robes than the other monks. He had a full beard, soft eyes, and a warm, if melancholy, smile. I knew we'd been afforded a rare honor. The Atang seldom appears in public, and as the most honored priest of the Ethiopian Orthodox Church, he *never* leaves the chapel compound. A prisoner of his own spiritual virtues, he will serve the remainder of his life within the one-acre compound.

Before Birani allowed us to ask questions, the Atang prayed a blessing over each member of our team, wetting our heads with holy water from a tarnished pewter chalice and gently placing his silver cross on our foreheads, cheeks, and lips. Startled villagers pressed in around us, seeming agitated, even angered, to see their holy man lavishing blessings on foreigners.

"The guardian has agreed to meet you only because of your heart for our people," Birani whispered to me. "You may now ask him your questions."

How does one address the only living person reportedly allowed to see the ark? I didn't know, so I eased into it, introducing myself and explaining why we had come to Axum. Then I noted respectfully, "Esteemed guardian, to hold a position of such great honor, you must feel privileged."

"Yes, it is a privilege," he said, speaking in Tigrigna. Then he lowered his eyes with a trace of resignation, "Yet it is also a heavy burden."

Having set himself apart from youth with an exemplary life— manifested in love of God, purity of heart, and cleanliness of mind and body—it became the Atang's unsought blessing and curse (as it has been for all guardians, past and future) to be chosen "guardian of the ark." Such great honor, however, did not always outweigh the burden of spending the rest of his life shut off from friends and family or forsaking all earthly distractions in order to stay at his post perpetually.

113

I had read an account of a former guardian, who, learning of his selection, fled to the hills. Brought back forcibly, he surrendered to the inevitable, finally embracing the most exalted position in his country's religious hierarchy.

I looked into the Atang's eyes and thought I recognized a glint of sadness. What a sacrifice never again to walk the hills of one's youth or linger over long summer afternoons with friends and family! The Atang had lived a virtuous life, and for that he now ministered before an object that he—and others—believed to be an instrument of God's ineffable will. With a gentleness I found remarkable, even for a man of the Atang's spiritual capacities, he said he had long ago made peace with his fate.

"It is not for my own happiness," he said, "but for God's pleasure that I occupy this position."

Here I wondered at the nature of a job that seemed to generate so little joy. It occurred to me, perhaps wrongly, that if the Atang truly ministered before the original ark, then God's presence must not dwell about the object in the same fullness and intensity as in Old Testament times; otherwise, these diligent servants might find more jubilation in their calling.

At last I posed the question I'd been longing to ask: "Honored guardian, I have come to ask you in person: Do you truly guard the original ark of the covenant?"

"Yes," he said, "we have the ark."

"May I ask what it *looks* like?" His well-rehearsed answer echoed similar accounts I'd read.

"As it is described in the Bible, so it is," he said mechanically. "King Solomon placed the ark in the Holy of Holies of the temple that he had built in Jerusalem. From there it was removed and brought to Ethiopia."

As I prepared to ask him specifically about its features—the configuration of the cherubim, its exact dimensions—the Atang raised a hand, halting all questions. With a smile he politely excused himself, bowed lightly, then turned to walk back up the steps into the chapel.

"I guess the interview is over," I said to Brandon, as we watched the guardian drift up the steps and disappear behind the iron-reinforced door. Our session had ended as suddenly as it had begun. We gathered our gear and walked back across the grounds toward the hotel.

Before we had gone far, Birani came alongside and whispered: "Mr. Bob, there is an old man in town, a former church administrator who still lives near the chapel. I believe he might have information about the ark. If you are interested, he might be willing to talk with you. I can arrange an introduction."

This tip, I knew, had come only because of my developing relationship with Birani. We now considered ourselves friends; I had demonstrated something more than American adventurism, and he had chosen to take a chance on me.

According to Birani, the elderly priest, once charged with indoctrinating new guardians into the details of ark (and chapel) maintenance, had in his heyday held an esteemed position within the monastery. Whenever an Atang died, this man taught the new Atang how to light the incense burners, conduct the cere-

monies, and care for the ark. It all seemed fishy to me—I thought
only the guardian ever tended to the ark—but I hesitantly agreed.

"OK, Birani," I said, "I'll meet your monk."

ANOTHER EYEWITNESS TESTIMONY

Birani led us down a shady lane through a thicket of over-
hanging brambles and olive trees, to a small hutch on the
periphery of the church compound. There we found an old man
sitting on a stump beneath the branches, reading his *Ge'ez* Bible.
By his look—sun hardened, with shriveled features and a distant,
cloudy stare—he had to be at least one hundred years old. Birani
introduced us, then nodded for me to proceed.

I asked the old fellow straightaway if he'd ever seen the ark,
and if so, why.

"I have seen it twice in my lifetime," he said in a whisper. "I
saw it while carrying out my duties, for ten minutes each time."

"What does it *look* like?" I asked.

He began to fidget, though his lifeless eyes grew wide and
alert. In soft, raspy Tigrignese he explained, "It looked to be a box
with winged angels overshadowing the lid. And it frightened
me."

"It frightened you?" I asked. "Why?"

"Because it moved."

"It *moved?* What do you mean, it moved?"

He repeated softy, "It *moved.*"

I waited a moment, then asked him to elaborate, but all he
could say is that it moved.

"My eyes glanced upon it on two occasions," he repeated,
"and it frightened me. I also saw two tablets of stone on a separate
pedestal within the sanctuary. Each tablet measured about two
inches thick; and their length . . ." he measured off a distance
from the tip of his finger to his elbow. "Each had a light brown
color."

"Were they the . . . ?"

115

"Yes," he interrupted, "they are the tablets."

I asked him to describe the dimensions of the box. He described an object approximately three and one-half feet long, by two and one-half feet high and two and one-half feet wide, surmounted by two figures of winged cherubim facing each other across a heavy golden lid—roughly the dimensions of the biblical ark. My adrenalin now surging, I scanned my mental checklist and asked another question.

"Could you describe the *color* of the box?"

He paused, then pointed to my gold wedding band. "It is lined inside and out with gold, the same color as your ring."

Whatever he had seen, it sounded a lot like the ark. I glanced at Birani, who stood by impassively. Then I asked the old priest, "Are you convinced you were looking at the *original* ark of the covenant?"

His sullen eyes, dark and opaque, sunken deeply in their sockets, suddenly flashed bright. Something in my question, or perhaps my tone, offended him. Duly challenged, he said, "Yes! I *know* it is the ark."

"How do you know?" I persisted.

"One *knows* when he stands before the presence of God," he replied.

I tried to coax the man into further elaboration, but he had tired and seemed uncomfortable at this last line of questioning. For all I knew, he may have violated a vow of silence in talking of such sacred things. The monastery had entrusted him for many years with certain of the ark's secrets; perhaps he had crossed a line of propriety in speaking with me. I thanked him for his time, placed a hundred-birr note in his hand, and we left.

Now I felt confused. I had no way of knowing if this old man spoke the truth, but something told me the monastery did not train its residents to lie. I had nothing else to go on, so I took it on faith that I'd finally secured a semidetailed description of the ark from someone who had actually seen it. In general appearance, it seemed to match the Bible's portrayal. That in itself underscored the need to obtain a more detailed rendering of the object's appearance.

By now one thing had become clear: for many centuries, an object—either the original ark of the covenant, or some relic that the Axumites *believe* to be the ark—has lain in state in a chapel in Axum.

HOW WOULD WE KNOW?

One thing continued to bother me. How would we know for certain, even given the opportunity to view the relic, whether it was the authentic ark? Even a thorough reading of Exodus provides only a general description of a gold box surmounted by cherubim. The Bible gives no serial numbers, no defining markings or registration papers, to confirm the ark's identity. What would set the original ark apart from a replica?

We are left to speculate and to make some educated guesses. Aside from its basic size and features, what is known about the ark? One prominent feature would have to be the quality of its workmanship.

The Book of Exodus tells us how God instructed Moses to commission one of the greatest, Spirit-filled artisans of the time to build the ark. The artistry of the ark should be breathtaking and, perhaps, unmistakable. Exodus explains that God appointed the "gifted artisan" Bezalel, of the tribe of Judah, to oversee the construction of the ark and the mercy seat, as well as every aspect of the tabernacle and sanctuary. This man, Scripture tells us, not only possessed extraordinary gifts but had also been endowed supernaturally to perform "all manner of workmanship, to design artistic works, to work in gold and silver and bronze, in cutting jewels for setting, in carving wood, and to work in all manner of artistic workmanship" (Exod. 35:31–33 NKJV).

In attempting to determine the ark's appearance, design, and workmanship, it is also worth recalling when it made its appear-

117
Λ

ance. At the time of their liberation from Pharaoh, the Hebrews numbered anywhere from one and one-half to three million strong and likely would have boasted some of the most skilled craftsmen in all of Egypt. Bezalel, like the rest of his brethren, had been enslaved in Egypt. Since we know that the Egyptians used both slaves and free men to fashion their treasures, we can assume that Bezalel's workmanship would at least match the level of artistry seen in Egypt's finest fifteenth-century B.C. artifacts, today exhibited at repositories such as the Cairo and British Museums.

The writer of Exodus minced no words when he said that Bezalel stood head and shoulders above all other craftsmen; the Bible places him among the best of the best of the region's artisans. God's holy anointing upon Bezalel would only have enhanced his natural skills.

We must conclude that the authentic relic would have to embody Bezalel's remarkable artistry. The handiwork found in King Tutankhamen's tomb might provide a reasonable comparison. The intricacy of its wood carvings, the delicacy of its gold overlays, and the detail of its hammered gold work give us a glimpse at the best of Egypt's gifted artisans. The enabling of the Holy Spirit makes it unthinkable that the Hebrews would have produced anything less.

It seems likely, then, that the original ark and the mercy seat would loudly declare their own authenticity. I can only assume that the sight of the ark's angelic sentinels would steal one's breath and rouse one's spirit and that the detail of its gold overlay and deftly hammered moldings would evoke a glory familiar only to those who ventured behind the Holy of Holies The ark would be a jewel cut to adorn the crown of Deity himself.

†WELVE

THE NEW JERUSALEM

Back at the Yeha, we loaded the van and drove to the airport, where four members of the Axum police met us. They said they intended to arrest us for failing to obtain local permission to distribute medicines in the village.

We had less than two hours until our flight out of Axum.

I showed the officers the permits that Dr. Gaba had obtained from the Ministry of Health and Safety, but they insisted we had broken the local law. Some months back, they said, another group had dispensed medicine in town; a few of the sick had bad reactions and died. Now they wanted to check all of our passports, baggage, and paperwork to ensure that we had had nothing to do with that debacle.

I told the police I would stay behind if they would let the others fly out to Lalibella. Brandon wanted to stay with me, but I convinced him to go, assuring him I'd be on the next plane. The police agreed and let the team board the aircraft. Then, with fifteen minutes to go before our plane left the runway, my papers checked out. They released me with angry, threatening warnings.

I counted it almost a trifle; I'd learned that, in these countries, one doesn't have to be doing something wrong to arouse police suspicion. Simply being an American and conducting biblical research evokes strong reactions and often arrest without cause. I rejoined the others on the rocky tarmac, and we boarded the flight to Lalibella. There we hoped to inspect some of the world's most sublime religious architecture.

120

LALIBELLA

Happy-go-lucky Misgana picked us up at Lalibella's modest airport, situated in a rugged plain 150 miles south of Axum. We rode a rickety bus from the airport high into the Mount Abune Yosef range, ascending by twisting, narrow roads and hairpin turns edging over broad, plunging canyons. An hour into our climb we reached the thatched-hut hamlet of Lalibella—once known as Roha—where, eight hundred years ago, a noble king fashioned a secret marvel.

Misgana booked us into the rustic but charming Roha Hotel, home to Lalibella's famed native "chicken dancers," then escorted us on a breathless tour of the town's fabled stone churches, a pilgrimage for Ethiopian Christians for the past thousand years.

King Lalibella (A.D. 1181–1221) built the eleven monolithic churches to serve as the crown jewel of the Zagwe dynasty and, some believe, to house the ark. Local tradition suggests he built them with the help of angels,[1] under orders from God, who told the young king-in-waiting in a dream to build "churches the like of which the world had never seen before."[2] Today these towering edifices seem almost superhuman in scale, workmanship, and concept, some lying almost completely hidden in deep trenches while others stand majestic in quarried caves. A bewildering labyrinth of tunnels and narrow passageways with offset crypts, grottos, and galleries connects them all, leaving modern engineers at a loss as to how a so-called "primitive" culture could have carved such immense, intricate shapes directly into the volcanic tuff.

JOSEPH OF THE BLUE NILE

From Lalibella we flew to Bahar Dar, where I took Brandon and our videographers on a quick tour of Blue Nile Falls, all raging clouds and violent plumes, filling the valley with its thunderous fury. Starting up the trail, we ran into a group of youngsters determined to carry our packs and cameras; one smiling young boy of about ten years, named Joseph, attached himself to me. He shadowed me into the tan, sun-bleached valley, pestering me all the while in broken English to let him carry my camera. I finally handed it to him.

As we crested the final rise overlooking the falls, a soldier in full camouflage gear appeared from the trail below. Carrying a rifle and radio backpack with a huge whip antenna, he strode up and began berating the young boy carrying my camera. *What's a soldier doing here*, I wondered, *so far south?* Ethiopia's long-standing border dispute with Eritrea still raged some hundreds of miles to the north, but I couldn't see how that conflict posed much of a security risk here, at the mouth of the Blue Nile. Certainly the river and dam provided much of the northern territory its water, and as such presented some concern. My guess was that the soldier had been hired by the tourism ministry to shield tourists from pestering packs of trail urchins.

The soldier kept shouting at the terrified Joseph, becoming angrier with each burst of profanity. He finally started slapping the child in the head with wide, arcing blows. I didn't know how to respond. Even over the roar of the falls, the open clap of his hands made a hideous pop on the boy's head and face.

121
A

After a few seconds of this, I jumped between the soldier and the boy, blocked the next swing, and said something on the order of, "You hit that boy again and I'll . . . I'll . . ."

Once again, in a totally alien corner of the planet, I found myself squared off with an armed soldier, his startled yellow eyes fixed on mine, probably trying to decide whether he should arrest me or shoot me. Several moments of awkward silence followed, the irate soldier still holding the boy by the scruff of his neck; me holding the soldier by his greasy arm. Misgana and the other tourists stood to the side, no doubt holding their breaths.

Finally, with an angry snort, the soldier released the boy, who instantly disappeared into the brush. I stepped back, leaned down to grab my camera, and started walking down the trail, as if nothing had happened. I chose not to look back but expected at any moment to be stopped or arrested. I waited for the inevitable whistling sound of a bullet over my shoulder. It never came. And I never turned around to see what had become of the soldier or young Joseph.

RETURN TO TANA KIRKOS

From the falls we drove back to Bahar Dar and promptly hopped a boat back to Tana Kirkos, arriving at length at the smooth, green-water lagoon beneath the granite cliffs. Hurrying up the stone steps toward the village, we met an unusually animated Abba Baye rushing down to meet us.

Abba greeted me with a hug and a kiss on the cheek and instantly embraced Brandon as an honorary apprentice monk (promptly advising him on the advantages, spiritually speaking, of growing out his stubby beard). Abba escorted us back up to the village where we exchanged happy greetings with the other monks and boys, then quickly climbed up to the stone ledge and the altar of the ark. There we began videotaping and measuring the socket holes and columns.

After two hours on the ledge, we walked back down the path to the village. I felt relieved to have captured the site on film. We stopped as Abba stretched out his arm and pointed to a long, narrow fissure in a rock wall, which he said contained the skeleton of one of the original Hebrews who brought the ark to the island more than two thousand years ago. (Here again, a budding friendship yielded unexpected fruit.) It had been the custom back then, he said, to stuff the dead into one of the island's huge, V-shaped cracks and cover them with rocks.

I walked over and stared into the crack, packed top to bottom with heavy rocks. Carefully reaching my hand inside, hoping to snag an old artifact or whatever remained of the skeleton, I felt something soft, like fabric. I pulled it back to see (to my horror) that I held a large, molted snake skin. Thinking it alive, I jerked my hand from the crack, lacerating my knuckles.

"No more dead men in cracks," I playfully scolded Abba as we returned to the village to interview the monks about the so-called temple vessels—the basin, stand, and meat fork—which Abba promptly laid out for us on a mat. After an informative taping session, we boarded the tiny skiff and headed south to Bahar Dar to commence another long journey home to the United States.

123

Part Two

A FUTURE ROLE FOR THE ARK?

Thirteen

ALONG THE RIVERS OF CUSH

The body of circumstantial evidence, tradition, even coincidence, whispered that the ark had been taken from Jerusalem by Levite priests sometime during the reign of Manasseh; from there it spent two hundred years in Egypt, in a Hebrew temple on Elephantine Island, before traveling down the Nile and Takazee rivers to Tana Kirkos Island on Ethiopia's Lake Tana. Eight hundred years later, as the country converted to Christianity, King Ezana spirited it off to Axum, where it remains to this day.

My research in Israel, my travels to Elephantine Island, and my observation of ancient, oxidized trumpets, basins, stands, and meat forks—all of which matched biblical specifications—helped me formulate my conclusions. I had seen the ancient stone ledge where Tana Kirkos monks assured me the ark had sat, beneath a Hebrew-style tabernacle, for eight hundred years. I had touched peg holes in stone, where I judged the shafts of the tabernacle had been planted. I had run my hand along the rough surface of a stone obelisk believed to have been a Hebrew sacrificial altar. I had probed the tomb of a so-called Levite holy man believed to have been among those who brought the ark into Ethiopia. I had interviewed monks—including the Atang—who each swore to the ark's existence in Axum, and queried a retired priest who said he had more than once gazed upon the holy relic. This fellow still shuddered when he told me it "moved." Finally, I had toured the amazing stone churches of Lalibella.

I had seen and heard many things, and I had failed to find a single Ethiopian who offered anything but a full endorsement of his country's proud ark tradition. In the course of many months, I produced my own video on the subject; I continued reading, researching, and following up new leads.

Yet still I felt distant from the true object of my mission.

When Ethiopia yielded little more than what already had been dislodged, I retired to my office in Colorado Springs, ready to let the issue lie dormant. Until something else significant rose to the surface, I told myself I had no plans to return.

THE DOUBTFUL PROFESSOR

Sometime during this period I met a man who would help me begin to answer some of my questions. Ken Durham, at the time an assistant professor of biblical studies at a Christian college in Colorado, had heard one of my radio interviews about my earlier Mount Sinai discovery. Like so many others, he marveled at the theory and took the initiative to contact me suggesting we get together to exchange information regarding the exodus. I agreed and took an instant liking to this low-key, well-spoken, committed Christian professor, who, unlike many academics today, believes wholeheartedly in the inerrancy of Scripture.

In months to come our friendship grew. Here and there Ken began volunteering his time, helping BASE with research on specific search and recovery projects. Some months later, as our relationship evolved, I retained him as a consultant for BASE, handing off some research tasks that allowed me to focus more on search and exploration.

Through all the months, and in all our conversations, I had barely mentioned—in any detail at least—my musings on the ark of the covenant. One day I mentioned to Ken a verse that I had been brooding over for some time. I had always felt that Isaiah 18 read like an illustrated travelogue of northern Ethiopia (the biblical Cush):

> Woe to the land of whirring wings
> along the rivers of Cush,
> which sends envoys by sea
> in papyrus boats over the water.
> Go, swift messengers,
> to a people tall and smooth-skinned,
> to a people feared far and wide,
> an aggressive nation of strange speech,
> whose land is divided by rivers. . . .
> At that time gifts will be brought to the LORD
>   Almighty
> from a people tall and smooth-skinned,
> from a people feared far and wide,
> an aggressive nation of strange speech,
> whose land is divided by rivers—
> the gifts will be brought to Mount Zion, the place of
>   the Name of the LORD Almighty
>   (Isa. 18:1–2, 7).

129

It was clearly a prophetic verse referring to the ancient land of Cush—though prophetic to *what*, I couldn't say. *Cush* I knew simply as a Hebrew term referring to a nebulous territory that had, in the earliest Greek editions of the Bible, been translated as "Ethiopia." The Greek word *Ethiopia* means "burnt faces," while the Hebrew term *Cush* at one time referred to the entire Nile Valley south of Egypt, including Nubia and Abyssinia.[1] Today most scholars agree that Cush most likely applied only to the northern half of modern Ethiopia.

For reasons that remained unclear, I had always held the verse in particular awe. With its rich imagery of papyrus boats and smooth-skinned natives, it seemed an arresting picture of a land I'd come to love. The Ethiopia I knew easily qualified as a place of "whirring wings," evoking, for me, the disgusting swarms of flies and mosquitoes we'd always encountered north of Addis Ababa. Others attribute the verse to giant locust swarms that devour Ethiopia's fields and farms every decade or so.

Likewise, Cush's "papyrus boats" conjured up the Ethiopian *tankwas*, or papyrus canoes, made by the shoreline natives of Lake Tana. And the native Ethiopians I'd observed were indeed tall and smooth skinned, whose glowing, chestnut-brown complexions recalled both European and Asiatic features. And no one could dispute that the country sat "divided by rivers," criss-crossing the mountainous land in the Horn of Africa. I had observed both the Atbara and Takazze rivers cutting a glistening swath through its hot desert highlands.

Through my years of research and travel, I'd come upon a handful of obscure treatises that made vague parallels between Isaiah 18, Ethiopia, and the ark of the covenant. Even without all the connecting pieces, however, it didn't take a master theologian to see that the ancient land of Cush/Ethiopia held a position of status and prominence in the Old Testament.

The most cursory reading of the Bible reveals frequent references to Ethiopia/Cush as a place of whirring wings; mighty rivers; a tall, smooth-skinned people; and an aggressive race with ties to Egypt and India. These references certainly fit the ancient Axumite kingdom, whose wealth, political influence, and culture stretched throughout the Middle East. An even closer examination of Cush in the Old Testament reveals an unmistakable relationship between Ethiopia and the Israelites, God's chosen people. In Numbers 12:1, for instance, we note a relationship dating back at least to the time of Moses. Here Moses' sister and brother, Miriam and Aaron, rebuked God's prophet, speaking "against Moses because of the *Ethiopian* [or Cushite] woman whom he had married; for he had married an Ethiopia woman" (NKJV).

The verse goes almost unnoticed within the larger context of the exodus, yielding no clue as to whether the controversial marriage occurred before or after Moses' marriage to Zipporah the Midianite. However, Flavius Josephus, in his *Antiquities of the Jews* (book 2, chapter 10), states that the mysterious Ethiopian wife of Moses had been a princess named Tharbis. Though precious little is known of this marriage, Josephus relates that it came about during Moses' early years when he was a commander in Pharaoh's army on a military campaign in Ethiopia. According to Josephus, Tharbis was wed to Moses in order to secure a crucial political alliance between Ethiopia and Egypt.

Could this union between Moses the Levite and Tharbis the Ethiopian have resulted in Ethiopian descendants of Moses claiming a right as heirs to the care of the ark? Any offspring from this union would have created a Levitical bloodline in Ethiopia, providing yet one more link between the ark and Ethiopia. It also would have given refugee priests sufficient motivation to migrate with the ark to Ethiopia.

TIES FROM ANTIQUITY

Elsewhere in Scripture we find additional clues about Ethiopia's role and significance in biblical prophecy. One can be found in the Book of Amos, when the prophet wrote in the eighth century B.C., "'Are not you Israelites the same to me as the Cushites?' declares the LORD" (Amos 9:7). Given the vast territory attributed to Ethiopia in that period, one might justifiably ask, "To whom did Amos refer when he mentioned Cush?" We know that during Amos's ministry (783 to 743 B.C.), the only area of northern Africa impacted by the Hebrew faith and an area which lay clearly within the region of Cush/Ethiopia, had been the Falasha homeland in the vicinity of Lake Tana. It might not be inconceivable, then, that by the eighth century B.C. (if not much earlier), a flow of Hebrews already had traveled southward through Egypt into the highlands of Abyssinia.

These fleeting biblical references point to some kind of an early relationship between Israel and the Abyssinian highlands. They may hint at successive waves of Hebrew migration over an immense span of time, perhaps as early as the tenth century B.C. and continuing until at least the fifth century B.C. Whether any of these emigrants brought with them the ark, it is likely that, on their arrival in the Lake Tana area, the Hebrews (and/or Levites) would have met some of their own kind. These pilgrims naturally would have intermarried with some of the oldest established inhabitants of Ethiopia—such as the great, ancient Agaw tribe of western central Ethiopia²—and converted them to the Hebrew faith.

Here again we can make another justifiable hypothesis: Suppose the ark had come into Ethiopia in the aftermath of Manasseh. Chances are it would have arrived to a welcoming party of people influenced by the Israelites who looked like native Ethiopians and spoke a native language. The most likely modern descendants of these people are the now fragmented Qemant and Falashas, the black Jews of Ethiopia, still living in the Abyssinian highlands around Lake Tana. Indeed, Old Testament customs and practices can still be observed there not merely among the Falashas but throughout Ethiopia's Amharic Christian populations.

Even without Isaiah 18 and its whirring wings and papyrus boats, Scripture paints a lively picture of regional, cultural, and religious intercourse between ancient Israel and Ethiopia. How it impacted the search for the ark of the covenant would soon come into clearer focus. Moreover, as I would soon discover, the link between these two cultures had far-reaching prophetic overtones.

132

Fourteen

A GIFT FROM ETHIOPIA

While I found it interesting that seven-xteenth-century Portuguese Jesuit Balthazar Tellez had boldly asserted that Hebrews had lived in Ethiopia "from the beginning,"[1] and while I wondered at Isaiah's description of Cush as a place of "whirring wings" and papyrus boats, I had another, more pressing question for Ken.

What, exactly, did Isaiah mean when he predicted, "At that time *gifts* will be brought to the LORD Almighty from a people tall and smooth-skinned, . . . the *gifts* will be brought to Mount Zion, the place of the Name of the LORD Almighty" (Isa. 18:7, emphasis added)? It appeared from this verse that *something* prophetic would happen in Ethiopia that would directly impact Jerusalem, commonly referred to in Scripture as Mount Zion. The whole passage merited further consideration, yet my specific question to Ken targeted the gifts.

"What gifts do you think Isaiah was talking about?" I asked. "What gifts will the Ethiopians bring to the Lord?"

Ken had been working on some other projects for me and had, at best, a casual knowledge of my interest in Ethiopia as the possible resting

y
z
133

∧

place of the ark. In fact, he had even casually mentioned that he did not believe the ark could be in Ethiopia. As it turned out, however, that was all about to change. The shift began when I pointed him to this verse and asked, "What do you make of it?"

"Bob," he reminded me, "I know you're researching the possibility that the ark of the covenant is in Ethiopia, but you need to remember that I'm not a big fan of that theory."

I didn't take offense and assured him that his skepticism didn't bother me. Dropping a printout with the verse circled on his desk, I merely asked him to look into it when he got the chance.

We didn't discuss the matter for several weeks, and, frankly, I hadn't expected it to resurface, when Ken walked into my office one morning and said, "Bob, remember that verse in Isaiah 18 you gave me a couple of weeks ago? It has really been gnawing at me. I started doing a little checking, and I think I've stumbled onto something pretty interesting."

"Yeah?" I replied, mildly surprised. "What've you got?"

He carefully spread his notes out on my desk, sat down, and launched into a serious, marvelously detailed presentation.

"First," he began, "like so many sections of Isaiah, this is God's message to a specific region and its people. Messages like this usually begin with God's warning or condemnation, then move on to a picture of God's plan for them in Messiah's future kingdom. In Isaiah 18, God is addressing the people who are 'beyond the rivers of Ethiopia.'" He glanced up from his notes, then continued: "Moreover, Isaiah speaks prophetically of a procession traveling to Israel following the Second Coming, when Messiah returns triumphantly to establish his kingdom on earth."

My ears perked up. "Go on," I said. Ken led me through a number of prophetic Scriptures in which Jesus himself promises he will return to a future, believing remnant of Israel to establish his righteous kingdom over Israel, through Israel, and over the whole earth. One of these, Matthew 19, states: "So Jesus said to them, 'Assuredly I say to you, that in the regeneration, when the Son of Man sits on the throne of His glory, you who have followed Me will also sit on twelve thrones, judging the twelve tribes of Israel'" (v. 28 NKJV).

Many other prophetic passages, of course, describe this glorious event (such as Dan. 7:13–14; Mal. 3:1; Mic. 5:2; Isa. 24:23). Yet tucked within the lines of Isaiah 18 lay several references to the same event: Messiah's ultimate conquest and return to rule and reign as God and King in Jerusalem.

"It's a series of events called the *day of the Lord*," he said.

He read Isaiah 18:3, which states "When a banner is raised on the mountains," then carefully explained how its imagery could easily be linked to a Messianic prophecy in Isaiah 11: "In that day the Root of Jesse will stand as a banner for the peoples; the nations will rally to him, and his place of rest will be glorious" (v. 10). And again, reading from Isaiah 18:3: "When a trumpet sounds, you will hear it," he flashed ahead to Messiah's return prophesied in Zechariah: "The Sovereign LORD will sound the trumpet" (Zech. 9:14). Then back to Isaiah 18:4 and the phrase, "I will take My rest" (NKJV).

"This parallels closely the phrase, 'and his place of *rest* will be glorious' in Isaiah 11:10 and other passages," he said.

Ken placed his notes on my desk and traced a finger down the page as if reviewing a checklist. "Bob, Isaiah 18 clearly refers to the day of the Lord. I've checked it out thoroughly, and it's obviously talking prophetically about Messiah's return and conquest." He pulled another set of notes from a binder and said, "Now look at *this*."

He opened to a passage from the Book of Ezekiel, in which the prophet, in an angelic vision, saw and recorded the precise measurements, features, and configuration of the messianic temple. Ezekiel's vision, almost neurotic in its detail, itemizes a painstaking sequence of events immediately following Christ's return. According to Ezekiel 43, Christ will rule from a messianic temple in Jerusalem and take his place on a throne:

> And the glory of the LORD came into the temple by way of the gate which faces toward the east. The Spirit lifted me up and brought me into the inner court; and behold, the glory of the LORD filled the temple. Then I heard Him speaking to me from the temple. . . . And He said to me, "Son of man, this is the place of My throne and the place of the soles of My feet, where I will dwell in the midst of the children of Israel forever" (Ezek. 43:4–7 NKJV).

It seemed plain enough: on that day the Lord would come into his temple and dwell with his people Israel forever. Yet, in an interesting twist, it also appears that Christ's own throne—"the place of the soles of My feet"—would reside *within* the Messianic temple. Never before in the Bible had another Hebrew king—David, Solomon, Josiah—ruled on a throne from inside the holy temple; always they executed their royal offices from within the palace.

In an interesting aside, 1 Kings describes the seven-year construction of God's temple in elaborate detail, then notes that Solomon's palace, twice the temple's size, took twice as long to build. The *palace* always housed the king's throne. Yet here in Ezekiel, we have Messiah coming into the third temple on the day of the Lord and ruling from there on his throne.

"Fascinating," I murmured, staring at Ken's notes. "I'm intrigued by the relationship Ezekiel seems to draw between the throne of Christ and the messianic temple. What do you make of that?"

Ken nodded and, rather than answer my question, noted how, in the Gospel of Matthew, Jesus himself confirms the existence of a latter-day, or third temple, which Ezekiel describes. When he spoke of the temple's future desecration by the antichrist

(Dan. 7:8; 9:27), Jesus said, "Therefore when you see the 'abomination of desolation,' spoken of by Daniel the prophet, standing in the *holy place* (whoever reads, let him understand), then let those who are in Judea flee to the mountains" (Matt. 24:15–16 NKJV, emphasis added).

"The holy place can only be associated with the temple," he said, flipping forward to 2 Thessalonians, where Paul states: "That Day will not come unless the falling away comes first, and the man of sin is revealed, the son of perdition, who . . . sits as God *in the temple of God,* showing himself that he is God" (2 Thess. 2:3–4 NKJV, emphasis added).

Here were two quick references to a third temple. The logic of the verses seemed inescapable: since there exists no temple in Jerusalem today, another temple will be built prior to Christ's return. Not only that, but in the days before Jesus comes in power and glory to execute judgment on the earth, this temple will be defiled by the antichrist.

"The good news is that Christ ultimately prevails, as we all know," Ken said. "Jesus will either cleanse and restore the temple defiled by the antichrist, or he will raise up a new temple for himself. Either way, he wins."

I silently recalled what I had always regarded as the Bible's most glorious Scripture: "'Behold, I send My messenger, and he will prepare the way before Me. And the Lord, whom you seek, will suddenly *come to His temple,* even the Messenger of the covenant, in whom you delight. Behold, He is coming,' says the LORD of hosts" (Mal. 3:1 NKJV, emphasis added).

Mulling over these hopeful verses anticipating Christ's glorious reappearance and his coming into his temple and sitting on his throne, I momentarily forgot what any of it might have to do with Isaiah 18.

"Where are you going with this, Ken?" I asked.

137

"Watch this," he said. He flipped back to Isaiah 18:7: "At that time gifts will be brought to the LORD Almighty from a people tall and smooth-skinned."

He closed the Book and said, "This verse categorically states that, at the time of Christ's triumphant return to his messianic temple, *gifts* will be brought to Mount Zion from *Ethiopia*. Furthermore, these gifts will be brought to Mount Zion to the place of the 'Name of the LORD Almighty'" (Isa. 18:7).

Then he looked at me and asked, "Where do you think he means by the 'place of the Name of the LORD Almighty?'"

138

I shrugged. "I could take a guess, but why don't you make it easier on us both and just tell me?"

Ken then began describing how, during his study of the Hebrew text of Isaiah 18 and a number of cross references, he thought he had noticed a pattern, something laced through Scripture that had never crossed his mind. Where exactly *was* "the place of the Name of the LORD Almighty"?

"If what I'm seeing is true," he observed, "we may well be framing the larger purpose and whereabouts of the ark of the covenant in these latter days in an entirely new context."

I listened, deeply engrossed, as Ken walked me through passage after passage confirming that the place of the "Name of the LORD" had, in Scripture, always been intimately associated with the holy temple. Moreover, by tracing this phrase from Deuteronomy to Jeremiah, this place where the Lord's name could forever be found just happened to occupy the space directly above the ark of the covenant, within the Holy of Holies.

"*What?*" I asked, instantly aware that such a place also described the space between the wings of the cherubim on the mercy seat.

Ken turned back to the Old Testament and explained how the dwelling place of God's name was progressively revealed over time, from a broader meaning to a more specific usage, as God narrowed and further specified his revelation to Israel. In

Deuteronomy, for instance, the writer begins by identifying the place of God's name in the broadest possible terms, calling it "the land" he promised to his people (Deut. 12:10–11). In Jeremiah 7, God recalls the past and states, "But go now to My *place* which was in Shiloh, where I set My *name at the first*" (Jer. 7:12 NKJV, emphasis added). Here God referred to where the ark originally had been kept—that is, within the tabernacle at Shiloh (Jos. 18:1). Finally, we trace this forward to 1 Chronicles 13:6, where we are told: "David and all Israel went up to Baalah, to Kirjath Jearim, which belonged to Judah, to bring up from there the ark of the God the LORD, who dwells between the cherubim, where His name is proclaimed" (NKJV). In Ken's estimation, this final verse conclusively established the "place of his name" as residing above the ark of the covenant, stationed between the cherubim in the Holy of Holies.

Suddenly the conversation became more interesting. As we continued to track the "place of my name" terminology throughout the Old Testament, the passages consistently referred not only to the holy temple but also to the Holy of Holies within the temple.

There could be no mistaking it: God's name would dwell in the temple forever: "And the LORD said to him: 'I have heard your prayer and your supplication that you have made before Me; I have consecrated this house which you have built to *put My name there forever*, and My eyes and My heart will be there *perpetually*'" (1 Kings 9:3 NKJV, emphasis added). More than that, it would dwell forever in the Holy of Holies within the temple. Only one other item had ever been permitted within the Holy of Holies: the ark of the covenant.

Ken wore a cautious expression as, once again, he turned back to Isaiah 18:7—and *gifts* will be brought to "the place of the Name of the LORD Almighty."

"There's no mistaking it, Bob. This verse is talking prophetically about gifts from Ethiopia being brought to the most holy

139

place in the third temple." He paused, wary of my response. "Can you *see* it, Bob? We're talking about gifts being brought directly into the Holy of Holies of the temple, where the ark once resided . . . on the day of the Lord."

I could see where Ken intended to go with this, though I had no intention of letting myself get carried away. "OK, Ken," I said, "what kind of gifts?"

Ken answered, "Well, I checked the Hebrew on this word *gifts* in verse 7. And strangely enough, in this passage the Hebrew word *gifts* actually translates to 'gift.' It's singular, Bob. If I'm reading this right, one—and only one—important gift will be brought out of Ethiopia at the return of Christ."

At that we both went silent. I imagined bold, colorful images of Axum monks marching in procession to Jerusalem with some ultimate, incomparable gift or offering. I had never heard or read of such an event in all my travels or research. Anticipating my thoughts, Ken broke our silence: "Isaiah seems to be telling us that a significant, singular gift will be brought in procession to Israel from Ethiopia when the Lord returns to his messianic temple." He paused, then added, "According to verse 18, biblical prophecy tells us this gift will be brought to the place of the 'name of the LORD of hosts,' to 'Mount Zion,' which *must* refer to the most holy place in the messianic temple" (NKJV).

Spellbound, I barely heard Ken's next question, which he asked as slowly and deliberately as he could.

"Bob," he said quietly, "what is the *only* gift that could be worthy of being placed in the Holy of Holies of the messianic temple?"

Fifteen

THE MERCY SEAT

I found it more than a little ironic: the more aggressively we had tried to discount the ark in Ethiopia theory, the more evidence we kept digging up for something significant coming from Ethiopia to occupy the most holy place in the messianic temple.

The gift couldn't simply be a sacrifice, we reasoned, since sacrifices always had been made in the temple courtyard, outside the inner sanctum. No, it seemed from many Scriptures that a gift—singular—would be taken *inside* the temple. In our repeated dissection of Isaiah 18, we began to conclude that the gift would travel north from Ethiopia to Jerusalem sometime after Christ's return and wind up inside the holy place of the messianic temple.

Ken seemed almost obsessed by the subject.

"But now we've got a real problem," he cautioned me. "I can't get away from Isaiah 18:7, which refers specifically to Messiah's conquest and of a singular gift being brought from Ethiopia to Jerusalem by the people of Cush. This confronts us with an extremely significant scenario, coming as it does in conjunction with Messiah's return and conquest."

We tested and retested this thesis and found that the biblical phrase had referred respectively to the land of Judah, to the holy city of Jerusalem, to the Temple Mount, to the temple, to the most holy place within the temple, and ultimately, to a place located distinctly "between the cherubim" above the ark itself. I didn't need to be reminded that this could only refer to the mercy seat that covered the ark.

142

"Obviously," Ken continued, "following Messiah's return and conquest, one incredibly important gift is going to be brought to the place of the name of the Lord of hosts, which *has* to be the Holy of Holies in the third temple, the place where God's presence always had been synonymous with the ark of the covenant."

THE ROYAL PROCESSION

It turned out, much to our amazement, that Scripture contained many references to these events. In the Book of Zephaniah, for example, we found a passage that seemed a curious parallel to Isaiah 18. As the Lord prophesies his own triumphant return, he says: "'Therefore wait for me,' declares the LORD, 'for the day I will stand up to testify. I have decided to assemble the nations, to gather the kingdoms and to pour out my wrath on them—all my fierce anger'" (Zeph. 3:8).

Then the passage states, "From beyond the rivers of Cush my worshipers, my scattered people, will bring me offerings" (Zeph. 3:10). The New King James Version offers this translation: "From beyond the rivers of Ethiopia My worshipers, the daughter of My dispersed ones, shall bring My offering."

Once again Scripture provides a snapshot of events following the day of the Lord. The sequence begins with the pouring out of Messiah's wrath on the nations gathered against him, followed by an "offering" brought to him from "beyond the rivers of Ethiopia."

"Here we find the same pattern," Ken observed. "The offering described is also singular. God's worshipers will bring him a *gift*."

Even more intriguing than the imagery of the gift became the Hebrew meaning of the word *bring*. The term in Zephaniah 3:10 doesn't normally indicate a typical offering. The Hebrew word, in fact—cited both in Isaiah 18 and Zephaniah 3 (*yabal*)—differs vastly from the common term (*bo*) in that it implies a bringing or leading forth *in an official or royal procession* (Job 10:19; 21:30; Ps. 45:14–15; 68:29; Isa. 18:7). As Ken sat at his computer, he tapped out a few more commands, then looked up.

"Bob," he said, "these passages can easily refer to a royal or official procession. We apparently have a procession from Cush bringing forth something of a royal stature to Jerusalem, from beyond the rivers of Ethiopia."

We quickly realized this wouldn't be just *any* offering.

"The word used here is *minha*," Ken said, "and while it connotes a distinctly singular offering (as opposed to offering*s*), it also describes the various kinds of precious gifts and tributes brought into the presence of a human king by loyal subjects desiring to submit to and serve him." Staring at the screen, Ken added, "Bob, this is no common offering but appears to be one that would befit the stature of the Lord himself."

Now we had to retrace each step, trying to ensure we hadn't missed something.

"In Zephaniah 3," Ken repeated, "we have another unmistakable picture paralleling Isaiah 18, of Messiah assembling the nations and gathering the kingdoms in order to pour out his wrath and vanquish all of his enemies. And as in Isaiah, this, too, is followed by a royal procession from Ethiopia, bringing before him a singular offering of inestimable homage and tribute."

In simple terms Scripture was telling us that some incredibly significant event would follow Messiah's glorious entrance into Jerusalem. That event, it appeared, involved a royal procession from Ethiopia to present Messiah with a gift of great importance. This gift would be brought all the way into the place where his name dwells forever—into the Holy of Holies of the Jerusalem temple.

Given my own long-simmering assumptions about Ethiopia, it wasn't a huge leap for me at least to speculate on what that singular gift might be. What could be worthy of being brought all the way inside the temple to Messiah—especially since traditional offerings are always received *outside* the temple?

What, indeed, other than the ark of the covenant?

INTO HIS SANCTUARY

At this point we could hardly term our suspicions a "theory." Certainly we needed more supporting scriptural evidence to back up our hunch.

In one sense, the idea of what we now suspected seemed theologically radical and left us grasping for answers. What exactly would it mean—spiritually, logistically, eternally—for the ark of the covenant to be brought to the conquering Messiah in Jerusalem? And why would it be brought there? What would be its function? And what of the Scriptures that seem to challenge the existence of the ark?

On the one hand, I almost had to laugh. Within a matter of days, Ken had gone from being a skeptic of the Ethiopian hypothesis to becoming a strong proponent.

"Bob," he confessed, "after completing some serious word studies, I went from thinking the Ethiopian idea was a pretty flaky deal to being almost utterly convinced that the ark of the

144

covenant really *will* come out of Ethiopia. The thought of it knocked me off my feet."

Still, the obvious question remained: *Why?* What specific purpose would it serve?

In my gut I knew we had struck upon something of tremendous significance. And since I knew that nothing in the Bible can be deemed superfluous, I had to believe that God had a clear-cut reason for this revelation in Scripture.

From my standpoint, a first order of business had to be further examination of the single Old Testament verse that seems to question the ark's existence in modern times. Jeremiah 3:16 often has been used to argue against the ark's preservation. Jeremiah declares that any role for the ark in either the coming heavenly or earthly kingdom has long since passed:

> "In those days, when your numbers have increased greatly in the land," declares the LORD, "men will no longer say, 'The ark of the covenant of the LORD.' It will never enter their minds or be remembered; it will not be missed, nor will another one be made. At that time they will call Jerusalem The Throne of the LORD" (Jer. 3:16–17).

As I had discussed with scholars the aim of my travels into Ethiopia, this verse often came flying back at me with the force of a punch to the nose. "Before you go chasing after some fantasy," they'd warn me, "you have to deal with Jeremiah 3:16."

I never had a ready reply. I would simply shrug my shoulders and read off a checklist of my arguments for the ark's resting at Axum. Yet as Ken and I debated this verse, still willing to talk ourselves out of an exciting bit of conjecture, I kept bringing him back to the key point. *Why?* Why would men no longer say, "The ark of the covenant of the LORD"? Why would it never enter their minds or be remembered?

Ken had his suspicions, but I could see that he wanted to think things through before he attempted to articulate them. Our primary thesis now revolved around what looked to be an increasingly defensible scenario: that the "gift" spoken of in Isaiah 18 might indeed be the ark of the covenant, currently stored somewhere in Ethiopia; that it might be safeguarded there until such a time as the Lord's glorious return, when it would be transported in royal procession to Jerusalem; then it would be ceremoniously installed within the messianic temple's inner sanctum as the ultimate offering to the returning King. Our goal now seemed to be to disprove or affirm the theory.

For the next two weeks we buried our heads in stacks of Hebrew concordances, Bible software, and various other reference works, tracing the outlines of our theory back to its essence. All the while we suspected, with increasing confidence, that we had stumbled onto something that certainly livens up the discussion of modern prophetic understanding.

ABOVE THE MERCY SEAT

In the coming weeks it began to appear as if both the ark of the testimony and the mercy seat had distinct purposes in Christ's triumphal return. As new clues emerged, we assembled a substantial body of evidence to suggest that some purpose awaited the ark in the messianic temple. After much study and discussion, it began to look like Ethiopia might indeed play a prominent role in end-time events.

To bolster my own understanding, I found it necessary to dig more deeply into the background and symbolism of the ark and the mercy seat. While I had a basic knowledge of events surrounding these objects, I needed to understand fully their specific role and placement within the tabernacle and temple.

I understood that the glory of God's presence had frequently filled the temple. Yet I still failed to grasp how these objects served not simply as a physical interface between God and his people but as an earthly mirror of a heavenly reality. By reviewing the history of the exodus, I began to understand the role the ark and the mercy seat played in the tabernacle during the exodus and later in the temple.

We know that God placed the Hebrews in Egypt to multiply them into a great nation. We also know he redeemed them through the Passover and the exodus so that they might be his own possession. He led them to Mount Sinai and there gave Moses the law and directions for creating the tabernacle, the ark, and the mercy seat.

God instructed Moses to make an ark of acacia wood, overlaid with pure gold (Exod. 25:10–11), and ordered him to "put into the ark the Testimony, which I will give you" (Exod. 25:16). Then he instructed Moses to make a lid of pure gold, with two cherubim of hammered gold on top, their wings stretching over it and their faces looking down on it (Exod. 25:17–21). From above the ark, God said, "I will meet with you, and I will speak with you from above the mercy seat, from between the two cherubim which are on the ark of the Testimony, of all things which I will give you in commandment to the children of Israel" (Exod. 25:22 NKJV).

The ark contained the law, "the two tablets that Moses had placed in it at Horeb" (2 Chron. 5:10), otherwise known as the Testimony. The law always represented the presence of God's absolute righteousness in the midst of Israel (Rom. 10:5; 7:12).

Next God addressed the sin and guilt of his people. Because of his own holiness, God could not reign and rest among them until his wrath against sin had been satisfied. In a foreshadowing of Christ, God's wrath required a sacrifice—a sacrifice that could be satisfied only by the blood of an animal killed in place of the sinner. And since God's presence manifested above the ark, between the wings of the cherubim—as if he were sitting on a throne—the ark itself had to be sanctified with blood (Lev. 16:15).

By reading about this ritual in many translations, we began to take note of the distinctive method of this crucial sprinkling. Leviticus 16 (among many other passages) always describes this sprinkling of blood as taking place, first, in front of the mercy seat (where the feet of an enthroned ruler would touch the ground) and then on the mercy seat itself (where a ruler would sit on his throne).

We had skimmed these verses many times, but now the imagery leapt out at us. We began to see the ark and the mercy seat as the literal, physical focus of God's presence among his people. We knew that God came to rule as king, but we hadn't considered that, throughout Scripture, the king always sits upon a throne.

The gripping word-picture of God's voice emanating from "between the two cherubim" and "above the mercy seat" (Num. 7:89 NKJV), solidified the portrait of an invisible God sitting on his throne and executing the affairs of his kingdom.

This imagery can be seen most poignantly in the details of the atoning sacrifice. Once the blood atonement had been made, with the purifying sprinkling of blood both in front of and on the mercy seat, God assumed his place on his throne—the mercy seat! In a most literal sense, according to these verses, God's physical throne on earth always had been the mercy seat, located in the most holy place in the tabernacle.

That leads to the question, where did the term *mercy seat* originate? The fact is, the English term *mercy seat* is not a literal translation of the Hebrew word *kapporeth*. The Hebrew term—more literally "propitiation"—has long been debated among scholars. It seems to have little to do with the concept of mercy and apparently doesn't describe a seat. The *Theological Wordbook of the Old Testament* states, "The translation 'mercy seat' does not sufficiently express the fact that the lid of the ark was the place where the blood was sprinkled on the day of

148

atonement. 'Place of atonement' would perhaps be more expressive."[1]

In fact, the term *mercy seat* came to us from Martin Luther through the English Bible translation of William Tyndale. As such, it falls somewhat short of the author's original intent. In both ancient Egyptian and Hebrew thought, propitiation denoted the satisfaction of justice or wrath through the execution of punishment on a substitute. What distinguishes the term in connection with the ark is that it denotes not only the *act* of "ransom" or "propitiation" but also the *place* where such a benefit was accomplished. It described the one place (the mercy seat, or atonement cover) where the divine act (atonement or propitiation) occurred, allowing God to meet with his people, speaking to them from his shrine or throne. Once the act of propitiation (the sprinkling of blood before and on the mercy seat) had been accomplished, God could then "abide," "rest," or "meet" with his people and speak to them "from above the mercy seat . . . from between the two cherubim" (NKJV).

Therefore, even though the term *mercy seat* fails to encompass the full scope of the Hebrew, it nonetheless paints a wonderful picture of what actually occurred there. The term *mercy seat* also vividly illustrates all that will ultimately be fulfilled when the Messiah proclaims from inside his temple, "This is the place of My throne and the place of the soles of My feet, where I will dwell in the midst of the children of Israel forever" (Ezek. 43:7 NKJV).

A SCRIPTURAL PUNCH LINE

Once I saw this truth, I couldn't get it out of my mind. The image soon became the punch line for our thought process. The throne metaphors kept coming—except they didn't seem to be mere metaphors but literal truths.

Zechariah, for example, provides a stirring account of the returning King as he reigns from his throne in the temple:

"From His place He shall branch out,
And He shall build the temple of the LORD;
Yes, He shall build the temple of the LORD.
He shall bear the glory,
And *shall sit and rule on His throne;*
So He shall be a priest on His throne,
And the counsel of peace shall be between them
    both"
(Zech. 6:12–13 NKJV, emphasis added).

Verses like these, and many others, seem to portray the mercy seat of the ark as the messianic throne. As I began looking for scriptural references to God's "throne," and began considering the mercy seat as something separate and distinct from the ark of the covenant, I noticed that during Israel's wilderness sojourn, the mercy seat (as God's throne in the tabernacle) shone through from the ark's earliest appearance.

In Numbers 10, I saw that whenever the Israelites followed God through the wilderness with the ark going before them, Moses would pray:

"Rise up, O LORD!
Let Your enemies be scattered,
And let those who hate You flee before You!"
And when it rested, he [Moses] said:
"Return, O LORD,
To the many thousands of Israel" (Num. 10:35–36
    NKJV).

Here was a crucial and intriguing clue: whenever the ark was moved, the words were uttered: "Rise up, O LORD! Let Your enemies be scattered, and let those who hate You flee before You!"

150

As I followed that clue, I discovered that Psalm 68 opens with almost the exact same words: "Let God arise, let His enemies be scattered; let those also who hate Him flee before Him" (NKJV). As I scanned Psalm 68, I saw verses that further talked about correlations between the sanctuary (v. 24), the temple in Jerusalem, and kings bringing gifts (v. 29), and Ethiopia who will quickly "stretch out her hands to God" (v. 31). What an incredible coincidence! This corresponded exactly with Isaiah 18 and Zephaniah 3, which specifically portray that at the triumphal return of Christ, a "gift" will be brought from Ethiopia to the place of the name of the Lord of hosts, to the temple in Jerusalem!

I realized I had uncovered a probable connection between Ethiopia and the throne of God; and I also knew the Bible must have evidence to yield on the matter.

As we retraced our steps through the Scriptures, we discovered that Moses' proclamation when the ark was moved was a vivid picture of a king leaving his throne and leading his people and then returning again to rest and reign on his throne in the midst of his people.

We then discovered that in 2 Chronicles 6:41, Solomon moved the ark into the temple with the words, "Arise, O LORD God, to Your resting place, You and the ark of Your strength" (NKJV). This seemed to link the ark with the temple as the place of God's throne. And it appeared to be yet another confirmation that the mercy seat was the throne of God in the temple.

As we looked again at Psalm 68, we discovered that the enigmatic phrase "Ethiopia will stretch out her hands to God" can literally mean, "Ethiopia will rush to God *bearing on her hands*."

And finally, we arrived at Psalm 132, which seemed to tie together the same "Arise, O LORD" statement (v. 8), the ark

151

(v. 8), the temple (vv. 5, 7), God's promise to David concerning Messiah (v. 10), and Messiah's eternal throne (v. 11).

With heightened interest we turned to the New Testament and found that Jesus used this supernatural imagery of God's holy throne when speaking prophetically of the Son of Man (Jesus himself) coming "in His glory, and all the holy angels with Him," adding, "then He will *sit on the throne of His glory*" (Matt. 25:31 NKJV, emphasis added).

We had to wonder: *When Matthew wrote this passage, had he understood the nature of Christ's throne? Did he perceive it to be a spiritual or a physical throne? Did he know what it would look like or understand its divine form and function?*

As all Bible apologists encourage others to do, we were simply seeking to allow Scripture to interpret Scripture. This process had convinced both of us, from a variety of angles, that Jesus the Messiah will one day rule and reign on the earth from Jerusalem, on Mount Zion, in the temple, in the Holy of Holies.

And as incredible as it sounded, the biblical evidence kept mounting to commend the mercy seat of the ark as the literal, physical throne of the coming Messiah.

Sixteen

ON EARTH AS IT IS IN HEAVEN

As Ken and I debated the issues, we kept asking ourselves, "Should we assume that a literal, physical throne of David will be established inside the temple at the advent of Messiah's earthly kingdom? And could this throne be connected to the mercy seat covering the ark of the covenant?"

The deeper we probed, the more Scripture seemed to endorse the idea. Once we knew what to look for, the Bible's throne references seemed to crop up everywhere. Yet we kept asking the question from different perspectives. If our theory had any merit (by now we had begun calling it a full-fledged theory), if prophecy indeed meant to alert us that the ark would be brought to Jerusalem following Messiah's return as conquering King, then what of its ultimate purpose? If Christ, by his crucifixion and resurrection, fulfilled all that had been prefigured by the ark and the mercy seat as the place of propitiation in the Holy of Holies, then what purpose might the relic serve, if *not* to be the mercy seat where the one who accomplished a final propitiation would sit enthroned?

THE ARK *AND* THE MERCY SEAT

Once more we turned to the design of the ark. We knew that some scholars reject any notion of the ark as a seat or throne simply because its primary function had always been as a chest to hold the tablets of the law. Yet Scripture clearly states that the ark of the testimony (the wooden box proper) and the mercy seat covering the ark had always been devised as two separate objects.

Exodus 25, for example, portrays the object as a gold-over-laid wooden box or chest, approximately two and one-half feet high, almost four feet long, and approximately two and one-half feet deep. The mercy seat, however—a solid gold, crowning lid—had been built to *cover* the ark. Forged into the mercy seat were two gold cherubim, wings extended, facing each other and looking at the focal point of the ark, where God sat "enthroned" (2 Sam. 6:2). Here his *shekinah* glory rested when the blood of the day of atonement sacrifice had been sprinkled. Early on, Scripture differentiates the mercy seat from the ark proper.

In Exodus 30, for example, the Lord instructs Aaron in the burning of ritual incense: "Put the altar in front of the curtain that is before the ark of the Testimony—before the atonement *cover* that is *over* the Testimony—where I will meet with you" (Exod. 30:6, emphasis added).

Likewise, *Vine's Expository Dictionary of Old and New Testament Words* describes the mercy seat like this: "It was not a mere part of the Ark. It was placed 'above upon the Ark' (Exod. 25:17–22; 26:34; 30:6; 31:7; 35:12; 37:16). It is never called 'the cover of the Ark' but is treated as something distinct. The Holy of Holies is called in two passages 'the place of the Mercy Seat' (Lev. 16:2; 1 Chron. 28:11), confirming that it stood as something quite more than a mere subordinate part of the Ark."[1]

THRONE OF MERCY

The ark and the mercy seat, then, were to be perceived as distinct and separately functioning components. With this in mind, we attempted to identify other verses that amplified the distinction. In Isaiah we found another prophetic parallel between the words *mercy* and *throne*.

Isaiah 16 states, "In *mercy* the *throne* will be established; and One [Messiah] will *sit on it* in truth, *in the tabernacle* of David, judging and seeking justice and hastening righteousness" (v. 5 NKJV, emphasis added).

As we proceeded to sift and cross-reference Isaiah 16, we saw that in forecasting Christ's triumphant return, the Bible anticipates both a literal and a figurative culmination of God's covenant faithfulness. This is foreshadowed by three specific events: first, a literal throne will be established; second, it will be established in the "tabernacle of David" (in full prophetic fulfillment of God's promise to David in 2 Samuel 7, the temple); and third, Messiah will literally sit on that throne. And how would that throne be established? In *mercy*!

Perhaps the term *mercy seat* was not such a bad translation after all!

This brought us back to the original question: what kind of throne could appropriately be set up in the temple? So far as we could tell from Scripture, nothing less than the mercy seat would suffice. Still it merited deeper reflection, for prior to the coming of Messiah, no type of furniture for sitting had ever been placed within the temple. Why not? Because, as Hebrews attests, the priests who ministered before the ark never rested: "Day after day every priest *stands* and performs his religious duties; *again and again* he offers the same sacrifices, which can *never* take away sins" (Heb. 10:11, emphasis added). The passage clearly states that the priests never sat down inside the temple, so no chairs or similar furniture were needed.

So in the absence of any temple seating, from what type of throne might Messiah, God in glorified human flesh, righteously interact with his people, as did the "invisible God" of Exodus (Col. 1:15) with the children of Israel? And where in the temple might such a throne be located? Our research had suggested the astonishing possibility that the unique part of the ark commonly known as the mercy seat might well be the only appropriate physical throne of Messiah. But that left us with a problem.

156

"What about the ark itself?" asked Ken. "For if the ark and mercy seat are to be brought to Jerusalem from Ethiopia at the advent of Christ's Second Coming, and if the mercy seat is to serve as the throne of Messiah in the temple, then what of the ark of the covenant, the box with the law? It would no longer be the *ark* as we—and Israel—have always understood it."

The Bible, it turns out, addresses this concern. Christ's incomparable sacrifice ushered in a new covenant and tore in two the temple veil that separated man from God (Matt. 27:51). The spirit of this "better" covenant would seem to render the ark proper (the wooden chest with the law) as a thing of the past.

So could the ark proper get set aside or completely done away with, even as the mercy seat assumed its place as the physical throne of Messiah? Such a radical notion would cast the quest for the ark in Ethiopia in a dramatic new light.

We might wonder whether exactly this distinction was in Jeremiah's mind when he prophesied twenty-six hundred years ago, "'Then it shall come to pass, when you are multiplied and increased in the land in those days,' says the LORD, 'that they will say no more, "The ark of the covenant of the LORD." It shall not come to mind, nor shall they remember it, nor shall they visit it, nor shall it be made anymore. At that time Jerusalem shall be called *The Throne of the LORD*, and all the nations shall be gathered to it, to the name of the LORD, to Jerusalem'" (Jer. 3:16–17 NKJV, emphasis added).

This text tells us that the ark *proper* may no longer exist. The wooden box containing the tablets of the law—always intended as a type of Jesus, the Word become flesh (John 1:14; Rom. 7:4–6)—has certainly ceased to be important. Therefore, "It shall not come to mind, nor shall they remember it . . . nor shall it be made anymore."

Yet the same passage immediately alerts us that, while the ark shall no longer come to mind, "*Jerusalem* [here equated with the temple?] shall be called The *Throne of the LORD*"! The passage powerfully suggests the notion we had come to suspect, that the mercy seat—an entity distinct from the ark—would in that final day resurface to fulfill its preordained role as the focal point of the cherubim's gaze: "And there I will meet with you, and I will speak with you from above the mercy seat, from between the two cherubim" (Exod. 25:22 NKJV).

As we studied further, we realized that there was one other possibility, that the ark would still exist but would no longer be the focal point of attention, as it serves as the "foundation" of the mercy seat, Messiah's throne. This may be vividly pictured in Psalm 89:14, which reads, "Righteousness and justice [the Law] are the foundation of Your throne" (NKJV).

Whether the ark itself will one day come into the messianic temple, serving in a place of honor even as Messiah takes his rightful seat between the "wings of the cherubim," remains a mystery. But it now seems plausible that even if the ark "shall no longer come to mind," the mercy seat may yet serve as the literal "throne of the LORD."

EZEKIEL'S VISION

To Ken and me the theory seemed to be gaining steam. The mercy seat of the ark would be brought up from Ethiopia to be installed as the throne of the returning King.

Yet even as the evidence mounted, we still could find no Bible passage that unequivocally stated that the mercy seat will become the throne of Messiah. Nevertheless, we couldn't ignore all the amazing clues already gathered, like Ezekiel's supernatural vision of Messiah's climactic return to Jerusalem:

> And the glory of the LORD came into the temple by way of the gate which faces toward the east. The Spirit lifted me up and brought me into the inner court; and behold, the glory of the LORD filled the temple. Then I heard Him speaking to me *from the temple*, while a man stood beside me. And He said to me, "*Son of man, this is the place of My throne and the place of the soles of My feet,* where *I will dwell* in the midst of the children of Israel forever" (Ezek. 43:4–7 NKJV, emphasis added).

158

Once more we find Ezekiel escorting us into the inner court, where we hear the voice of Messiah sounding from within the temple, proclaiming, "This is the place of My throne." Here again it must be noted that never in the history of Israel has the temple been recognized as a place for a royal throne. Many teachers of eschatology deduce that Messiah's throne must be established somewhere in Jerusalem, but they stop short of recognizing the only appropriate place for His throne is his Father's house, in the Holy of Holies. Nowhere in our research did we find anyone who has proposed the mercy seat as the only appropriate place of God's enthronement in the Holy of Holies. Yet the voice of Messiah himself, the Lord of glory, emanating from the messianic temple, confirms that his throne, indeed, will be located inside his house.

This would be the *eternal* throne that was promised to David in 2 Samuel 7:16, not merely a temporal throne such as David, Solomon, and the other human kings of Israel occupied. (Apparently, the original throne David sat on didn't last even one generation, since Solomon built a new throne for himself.)

If Messiah must sit on the "throne of David" *forever*, only the imperishable mercy seat would qualify.

Further, we recognized that the messianic temple in Ezekiel 43:7 as "the place of the soles of My feet" clearly hearkens back to the placement of the day of atonement blood not only *on* the mercy seat but *before* the mercy seat.

By now our eyes had begun to focus on biblical passages we never before fully understood. Verses formerly clouded with enigmatic images of heavenly kingdoms, angelic hosts, and eternal thrones suddenly jumped off the page, emerging as literal portraits of the Second Coming and Christ's physical enthronement in his earthly temple.

THE HEAVENLY REALITY

As we moved into the final stages of our research, Ken tested our theory on his college students. Whenever he broached the topic of the ark in Ethiopia, a handful of his more incisive students invariably asked, "How can the ark be on earth when the Book of Revelation says it is in heaven?"

We had wrestled with the same question and had a ready answer. Revelation 11 states:

> And the twenty-four elders who sat before God on their
> thrones fell on their faces and worshiped God, saying,
> "We give You thanks, O Lord God Almighty,
> The One who is and who was and who is to come,
> Because You have taken Your great power and reigned.
> The nations were angry, and Your wrath has come,
> And the time of the dead, that they should be judged,
> And that You should reward Your servants the prophets
> and the saints,
> And those who fear Your name, small and great,
> And should destroy those who destroy the earth.

Then *the temple of God was opened in heaven*, and *the ark of His covenant was seen in His temple*. And there were lightnings, noises, thunderings, an earthquake, and great hail" (vv. 16–19 NKJV, emphasis added).

A case might be made from these verses that God had removed the ark from the first temple and translated it to his celestial temple. Certainly it would be no great feat for God to transport an earthly object into his heavenly domain. Yet that is clearly *not* what the passage implies, for the passage also refers to a heavenly temple, and already we have established that the events at Christ's return revolve about an earthly temple in Jerusalem.

The Jerusalem temple stands as a copy or shadow of the heavenly temple. Just so, the earthly ark mirrors the "ark of His covenant" that John beheld in his vision. Each earthly item mirrors the heavenly reality. Revelation 11:19, therefore, should not be taken to imply that the earthly ark has been supernaturally translated into the heavenly realm, any more than the earthly temple has been supernaturally moved to heaven.

Such a pattern appears frequently in Scripture. The entire Levitical worship, in fact, arose from a heavenly pattern, as Hebrews says: "Priests who offer the gifts according to the law . . . serve the copy and shadow of the heavenly things, as Moses was divinely instructed when he was about to make the tabernacle. For He said, 'See that you make all things according to the pattern shown you on the mountain'" (Heb. 8:4–5 NKJV; see also Matt. 6:9; Exod. 25:9; Acts 7:44).

Our understanding of the ark and the mercy seat, then, must be filtered through this divine lens. Both ark and temple are earthly copies of a heavenly original.

We began to detect a free-flowing exchange of temple/throne images within the heaven/earth paradigm. For if in heaven God rules from his throne in his temple, as stated in

160

Psalms and if the ark in heaven sits inside the most holy place in the temple, as seen in Revelation, then we may safely conclude that the ark in heaven occupies the same place as God's throne in heaven. The eternal reality of the heavenly temple, then, tells us that the ark and throne in heaven occupy the same place and perform the same function. Both are literally and figuratively God's throne!

So then, if God's kingdom on earth is a copy of his heavenly kingdom, we ought to expect that the earthly ark (or mercy seat) and throne would occupy the same place and serve in the same capacity within the Holy of Holies of the messianic temple. Therefore, we conclude the mercy seat will become the divine throne.

This, in fact, seems to be what Jesus himself had in view when he instructed his disciples to pray, "Your kingdom come. Your will be done on earth as it [already] is in heaven" (Matt. 6:10).

Further, Zechariah 6:12–13 discloses that when Messiah rules on earth, he will reign from his throne in the temple, not only as God and King but as the ultimate high priest:

> Then speak to him, saying, "Thus says the LORD of
>   hosts, saying:
> 'Behold, the Man whose name is the BRANCH!
> From His place He shall branch out,
> And He shall build the temple of the LORD;
> Yes, He shall build the temple of the LORD.
> He shall bear the glory,
> And shall sit and rule on His throne;
> So He shall be a priest on His throne'" (Zech. 6:12–13
>   NKJV).

Levitical priests never rested within the temple, just as the kings of Judah never sat on a throne within the temple. But Jesus Christ embodies both roles, that of the ultimate High Priest and of the King of Kings. In him all that had been

161

foreshadowed in the earthly law and testimony finds its fulfillment. He will build the temple of the Lord in that day, and reign there as a Priest on his throne. He also will sit in the Holy of Holies, where the ark of the testimony once rested, and there rule as King. And according to all we have seen, the mercy seat will serve as his throne.

> All of these facets come together beautifully in Psalm 132:
> *Arise, O LORD, to Your resting place,*
> *You and the ark of Your strength.*
> Let Your priests be clothed with righteousness,
> And let Your saints shout for joy.
> For Your servant David's sake,
> Do not turn away the face of Your Anointed.
> The LORD has sworn in truth to David;
> He will not turn from it:
> *"I will set upon your throne the fruit of your body.*
> If your sons will keep My covenant
> and My testimony which I shall teach them,
> Their sons also shall sit upon your throne forevermore."
> *For the LORD has chosen Zion;*
> *He has desired it for His dwelling place:*
> *"This is My resting place forever;*
> *Here I will dwell, for I have desired it"*
> (Ps. 132:8–14 NKJV, emphasis added).

This awesome passage reveals, in the most moving terms, that the Lord's resting place is the same as that of the ark of his strength (v. 8)—in the Holy of Holies. In this sacred vestibule God the Father will place the fruit of David's body, the Messiah, to rule forever (v. 11). Messiah will sit on the throne in precisely the same place occupied by the ark of the covenant.

Can there be any doubt that the only appropriate place for all this to occur is in the most holy place of the messianic temple?[2]

Seventeen

ONE LAST HURDLE

We knew our theory that the mercy seat might one day serve as a throne for the returning Messiah faced at least one last hurdle, and it seemed a most practical hurdle indeed. What was the actual configuration of the cherubim overshadowing the mercy seat?

Most popular depictions of the ark have the angels' wings jutting across the top of the wooden box in an angular profile—almost like a gymnast's parallel bars—a formation that would make a most uncomfortable seat for a throne. We guessed, to the contrary, that the wings of the cherubim would have to thrust out, down, or over, in such a posture that a king could actually sit atop the relic.

So how did the cherubim's wings extend over the ark? Did they overshadow the top of the ark like a canopy, as seen in most Hollywood portrayals? Or did they extend upward or downward, or both, in some other motif?

BACK TO THE SCRIPTURES

Keeping in mind that the mercy seat had been built as an entity unto itself, perhaps for a specific purpose, Ken Durham and I had been searching Scripture to find clues about the most likely posture of the cherubim above the ark. Our search took us quickly to the Book of Exodus. In Exodus 25:17–21 we read that God ordered Moses to build the mercy seat of pure gold, instructing him to make two cherubim at the two ends of the mercy seat: "And the cherubim shall stretch out their wings above, covering the mercy seat with their wings, and they shall face one another; the faces of the cherubim shall be toward the mercy seat" (v. 20 NKJV).

After a few passes at this passage, we observed something interesting: for one, God did not go into great detail on how the wings of the cherubim should be positioned; He directed only that they should cover the mercy seat with their wings. Did their form not matter? Did God leave the design up to the artisans? If so, then what artistic influences may have informed early Hebrew craftsmanship?

Ken, who had researched something of both Hebrew and Egyptian art, suggested that artifacts discovered in the tomb of young King Tutankhamen might give us a clearer grasp of the appearance of the cherubim.

Many comparisons can be made between Egyptian and Hebrew artifacts of the period. Tut's treasures included an Egyptian version of an ornate, arklike box or chest, as well as several thrones. The most glorious of these came to be known as Tut's "golden throne," composed of a gracefully arranged collage of real and mythical creatures. Of course, these chests and thrones, while reminiscent of certain early Hebrew vessels and implements, had never been conceived as a unified representation of the king's presence (as the ark had). Still, in the absence of detailed instructions from God, the design techniques of the period may well have influenced the Hebrew artisans. One thing we know for certain: since the Hebrews lived in Egypt for four hundred years prior to the exodus, their assimilation into

Egyptian culture (and therefore its artistic tastes) would have been extensive.

While under no circumstances had it been God's purpose to mimic the idolatry of Egypt, the possibility still exists that once he gave his people the command to fashion the ark with winged beings facing each other on the mercy seat, they used their Egyptian experience to fashion a motif familiar to them. Inasmuch as the thrones of the Egyptian pharaohs had been configured of the living animals they worshiped, the throne of God (or the atonement cover) featured angelic beings, or cherubim, which Scripture tells us dwelt near his holy presence.

167

WINGS OF THE CHERUBIM

Theories about the appearance of the ark and the mercy seat have varied widely through history. Some renderings make it out to be an extravagant, thronelike structure, while others suggest little more than a modest box with a plain lid.

Some can't help but try to embellish the biblical description, which admittedly leaves out many of the finer details. Yet the Bible provides several clues. Consider Exodus 25:

> "You shall make a mercy seat of pure gold; two and a half cubits shall be its length and a cubit and a half its width. And you shall make two cherubim of gold; of hammered work you shall make them at the two ends of the mercy seat. Make one cherub at one end, and the other cherub at the other end; you shall make the cherubim at the two ends of it of one piece with the mercy seat. And the cherubim shall stretch out their wings above, covering the mercy seat with their wings, and they shall face one another; the faces of the cherubim shall be toward the mercy seat. You shall put the mercy seat on top of the ark, and in the ark you shall

put the Testimony that I will give you" (Exod. 25:17–21 NKJV).

The challenge in gleaning a precise description of the mercy seat lies in the multiple meanings of the original Hebrew. For example, the Hebrew word translated "stretch out" in verse 20 can also mean "spread," as one would spread a banner or cloth upon a table. Likewise, the term for "above" in verse 20, as in "they shall stretch out their wings *above*" (or "on high" in the King James), can suggest anything from "over" or "against," to "from above" or "upon" (the latter relating to a "downward" aspect). And the Hebrew word for "covering" used in verse 20 can also mean "overshadowing," "fence in," "cover over," "join together," or "hedge in."

Clearly, trying to determine the exact placement of the cherubim's wings could get complicated. No wonder a great deal of ambiguity persists about the true appearance of the mercy seat. Most English-language translations—most obviously the New International Version, in which the cherubim are said to "have their wings *spread upward*"—imply cherubim in a standing position, wings outstretched parallel to, or extended high above, the ark. This depiction gained broad circulation in the movie *Raiders of the Lost Ark*.

The problem with such an arrangement, for us, lies in the function we believe the mercy seat is yet to serve. As the physical throne of Jesus Christ, such a configuration simply wouldn't provide a sensible seat. So the question is, if the Lord meant the mercy seat one day to serve as a literal throne, then what should the cherubim look like? Does Scripture provide us with any clues to help us determine what may be possible in its design and appearance?

Up front, it's interesting to note that God went into some detail to specify the dimensions—length, width, and height— of the ark (or wooden box), yet the Bible gives only the length and width of the mercy seat: "You shall make a mercy seat of pure gold; two and a half cubits shall be its length and a cubit and a half its width" (Exod. 25:17 NKJV).

And what of the cover's height? Was its vertical dimension not worth mentioning? Most probably the omission signifies that the height of the mercy seat was of no practical consequence or that it was to be fashioned in such a low aspect that it need not be mentioned.

In fact, the Bible indicates, without explicitly telling us, that the mercy seat could not have been tall, bulky, or structurally complex. Exodus 25 gives us a clear description of the materials and methods used to construct the mercy seat, telling us, first, that its designers made it of "pure"—that is, non-alloyed—gold (Exod. 25:17). Pure gold, we know, has distinct physical properties; it is among the most soft and pliable of all metals. Any structure made from pure gold would necessarily be limited in size by its high pliability and low tensile strength. Pure gold is also heavy, meaning that the larger, or "taller," the mercy seat stood, the heavier it would be (and the less portable it would become). Remember, the Levites carried the ark and the mercy seat about on their shoulders, supported only by long poles.

It seems highly doubtful that the atonement cover could have been a large, cumbersome object. A solid gold structure of significant mass atop the ark would have made the unit almost impossible to carry easily, and we know the Levites carried the ark for long distances in their desert wanderings.

We also know that the cherubim on the mercy seat had been a "hammered work" (Exod. 25:18), requiring a metal sculpting method widely used in ancient times. The technique not only conserved costly materials but also limited weight and provided the greatest potential for creating delicate, natural features. It involved beating, or "hammering," thin sheets of metal around specially rounded forms to produce a light, three-dimensional figure or structure. The finished product typically consisted of a hollow, molded, masklike surface that looked solid but did not have the mass or weight of a solid image.

Again Pharaoh's treasures provide a reference point. The world's most famous work of hammered gold can be seen in King Tut's burial mask, on display in the Jewel Room of the Cairo Museum. Approximately twenty-four inches from top to bottom, the mask looks solid, when in fact it consists of two thin sheets of pure, beaten gold, molded, smoothed, then fused together around forms, producing an eerily realistic representation of Tut's young face.

Now the question becomes: did the Hebrew artisans forge the "hammered gold" cherubim flanking the mercy seat in the same fashion? Certainly no other technique would have allowed them to sculpt a comparatively lightweight, detailed representation of heavenly beings. Given the height and weight limitations of pure gold, probably only a hollowed-out, low-profile figurine would allow for both a fine, artistic rendering of the cherubim's wings while still making sound structural sense for an object that would be moved frequently over long distances.

Such a design seems to be exactly what the historian Philo imagined when he wrote of the mercy seat in the days of Paul and Jesus: "Its length and width are accurately described, but its depth is not mentioned, being chiefly compared to and resembling a geometrical [symmetrical] superficies [surface]; so that it appears to be an emblem [relief impression], if looked at physically."[1] Philo understood the mercy seat to be a low-lying, molded emblem, sculpted into an image of cherubim.

Such a low-profile motif supports our understanding of the mercy seat as the throne of God. Because the gold wings of the cherubim couldn't be made to stand upright to any significant height, they probably covered the seat more like a tablecloth.

With this image in mind, we can now revisit the Hebrew words found in Exodus and compare them with the physical properties of hammered gold. Such an exercise may tell us that a more natural posture for the cherubim's wings would be to blanket the mercy seat like a quilt, feathers spreading outward and downward from the cherubim's torsos and across the top of the atonement cover. (See an artistic rendering in the photo section, photo # 22.) Such an image of the cherubim's wings—flowing down from opposite sides and covering the mercy seat in a sloping, U-shaped arc, like the swaybacked spine of a suspension bridge—recalls a verse in Luke, directed at Jesus: "He will command his angels concerning you to guard you carefully; they will lift you up in their hands [wings], so that you will not strike your foot against a stone" (Luke 4:10; Ps. 91:11–12). Here again we have what might be considered a prophetic foreshadowing—a stirring vision of the Lord's presence being born aloft between the cherubim, on a throne composed of angelic wings.

171
Λ

Such a picture seems not only logical but also practical. Keep the image of the mercy seat as a portable throne in mind while reviewing Exodus 25:17–21 as it might appear, more literally rendered from the original Hebrew: "And the cherubim shall *stretch forth, from above,* their wings *against* the mercy seat, *covering over* or *hedging in* the mercy seat with their wings."

Such an understanding of the wings of the cherubim—fashioned from hollow, hammered gold and flowing down over the atonement cover like a blanket—support our theory of the mercy seat as a literal seat or throne. A sloping, U-shaped sling of angels' wings would support the presence of Messiah in the place where God abides and dispenses his mercy.

THE LORD REIGNS!

Arriving at our new theory regarding the mercy seat required us to weave together a mosaic of biblical clues; yet through our hours of interaction with the Scriptures, we slowly gave in to the apparent verdict: Following the victory of Jesus the Messiah, the ark and/or the mercy seat will be brought from

Ethiopia to Jerusalem, where it will serve as his throne in the Holy of Holies in the messianic temple. From there Messiah will reign as God and King in the place the Lord had always reigned in the midst of Israel—from the mercy seat.

This prophetic sequence of events, arriving in a form we could never have anticipated, yet drawn from Scripture, seems to fulfill every notable prophecy regarding the ark, the mercy seat, the temple, Israel, Jerusalem, Mt. Zion, Ethiopia, the Messiah, his priesthood, and his eternal rule. And it clarifies better than anything I've ever imagined what is perhaps Christianity's most transcendent promise: "When the Son of Man comes in His glory, and all the holy angels with Him, then He will sit on the throne of His glory" (Matt. 25:31 NKJV).

While we realize that some may deem our conclusions a drastic paradigm shift, nevertheless we present them for earnest biblical review and testing. They remind us, as perhaps never before, that the Messiah's kingdom *will come*, and his Father's purposes *will* be done on earth as it has always been in heaven.

> The LORD reigns;
> Let the peoples tremble!
> He dwells between the cherubim;
> Let the earth be moved!
> The LORD is great in Zion,
> And He is high above all the peoples
> (Ps. 99:1–2 NKJV).

Eighteen

THE ETHIOPIAN EUNUCH

Standing as we did on the shoulders of a radical new theory, I felt an urgency and excitement I hadn't known in years. To have scratched the surface of a prophecy of such magnitude evoked a rush of adrenalin like the one that hit me when I clambered off the treacherous heights of Mount Ararat in pitch darkness, with the Turkish army hot on my tail.

The body of Scripture supporting the mercy seat as Christ's throne not only made for a compelling story line but also began to elicit positive feedback from a handful of qualified theologians. After submitting our thesis to a select group of scholars, we found that while some spurned the idea, others were visibly enthusiastic. And no one could persuasively dispute it. This told us we had stumbled upon an important theme that might well stand up under rigorous biblical scrutiny.

By now we felt reasonably certain of the ark's role in prophecy. The wealth of biblical clues about Cush brought us back, full circle, to Ethiopia's ark tradition. Yet one final factor in the equation held us at bay. While we now believed that the ark and/or the mercy seat definitely would play prominently in the last days, there remained unsettled questions about Ethiopia's role in the pivotal affairs.

QUEEN CANDACE'S MESSENGER

By God's grace, over the course of weeks, we came upon another bombshell: a remarkable New Testament passage that not only hinted at the ark's future purpose and whereabouts, but one that also revealed how Ethiopia had, from the beginning, figured prominently in the gospel narrative.

The bombshell arrived in the form of a well-known passage in Acts, which, frankly, I'd always considered slightly misplaced. Yet now, trying to read between the lines, we came back to our central thesis and once more found Ethiopia at the forefront in the unfolding saga of Christ's return.

The story begins in Acts 8, where Luke records a significant encounter between one of Christ's disciples and an Ethiopian eunuch. To set the stage, let's travel back to Judea in the days following Christ's ascension.

Following the Holy Spirit's outpouring on the day of Pentecost and Christianity's first dramatic conversions, the early church began to grow. Thousands came to faith amid an atmosphere of miracles, signs, and wonders. The revival shook the religious leaders of the day, who regarded it a dangerous threat. A severe persecution broke out, scattering Christ's followers throughout Judea and Samaria. Yet the persecution only galvanized the new believers, who "preached the word wherever they went" (Acts 8:4).

Enter Philip, an early evangelist. He had traveled to Samaria to preach Christ, and miraculous signs and many conversions accompanied his sermons. In the course of his powerful missionary tour, an angel of the Lord appeared and instructed Philip to "go south to the road—the desert road—that goes down from Jerusalem to Gaza" (Acts 8:26). There the

174
Λ

evangelist met an Ethiopian eunuch returning home from Jerusalem.

Luke, the writer of Acts, identifies the Ethiopian as a prominent official in the court of Candace, "queen of the Ethiopians." The man managed her royal treasury and had come to Jerusalem to worship. (It is interesting to note that this terminology matches that used by Matthew 2:2 in referring to the journey of the Magi to honor and submit to Messiah.)

The eunuch had begun his journey home, when Philip, guided by the Holy Spirit, ran up to the chariot and overheard the eunuch reading from Isaiah 53. The passage, Isaiah 53:7–8, foretold the crucifixion of Christ. Most Christians know the rest of the story: Philip asked the eunuch if he understood what he read; and, informed of the man's confusion, Philip told the Ethiopian the good news of Christ. The encounter ended with the eunuch professing faith in the Savior, being baptized by Philip, and starting home to Africa in high spirits (Acts 8:39). In short order, the Spirit whisks Philip away, and the Ethiopian returns to Cush, no doubt to sow the seeds of Christianity throughout the Axumite kingdom.

The story gives us a wonderful glimpse at a telling moment in the expansion of the church into northern Africa. But here we need to step back and ask: was this Luke's sole intent? Perhaps not.

What if we view the entire episode in a slightly different light—say, from the context of Isaiah 18—recalling that, centuries earlier, Isaiah foresaw some great offering coming forth from Ethiopia at the Messiah's triumphant return? By adjusting the slide under this microscope, we might see an otherwise minor passage come into sharp focus. Seen through the lens of Isaiah 18, Philip's encounter on the desert road may become extremely significant.

WHY DID HE COME?

We know that the eunuch had charge of all of Candace's treasures (Acts 8:27). But why, other than to worship, had this particular Ethiopian traveled to Jerusalem during its holy feasts? And why, other than to offer a glimpse at the spread of Christianity's roots into surrounding regions, had Luke bothered to record it? Why did Candace send a eunuch, and why did he carry in his chariot a cumbersome, albeit valuable, scroll of Isaiah? Finally, why, when Philip appeared beside the chariot, are we told that the eunuch read from Isaiah 53? And could this episode shed light on the question of whether the ark and the mercy seat lay in Ethiopia at that time?

The answers we propose might come as a shock.

Isaiah 53, which accurately predicts the suffering and death of Messiah, immediately follows a passage in Isaiah 52 that includes a list of characteristics identifying the Messiah. Isaiah gives a description of Messiah's kingdom, along with a command to some group outside of Israel:

> The LORD has made bare His holy arm
> In the eyes of all the nations;
> And all the ends of the earth shall see
> The salvation of our God.
> Depart! Depart! Go out from there,
> Touch no unclean thing;
> Go out from the midst of her,
> Be clean,
> You who bear the vessels of the LORD
>   (Isa. 52:10–11 NKJV).

Take note of the phrase: "Go out from there . . . you who bear the vessels of the LORD." The phrase precedes Isaiah 53, which prophesies Christ's suffering and death. No doubt the Ethiopian viewed Isaiah 52 and 53 as they should be—as two

176
Λ

parts of a whole. Could he have received them as marching orders to make haste to Jerusalem to identify Messiah?

Could this verse be a clue alerting us to the eunuch's true motives for visiting Jerusalem? For if the ark and the mercy seat indeed lay hidden in northern Ethiopia, then no doubt both articles (or "vessels") had been registered among Candace's royal treasury. And if the monarch of Ethiopia considered those vessels a holy trust to be held until the arrival of Israel's Messiah, then the eunuch's purpose in visiting Jerusalem may well have been to determine whether the King's throne would now be required. Could the royal emissary of those "who bear the vessels of the LORD" have traveled to Jerusalem to confirm the identity of Messiah?

I recalled that in every interview with the Axum monks, as well as with those on Tana Kirkos Island, all had readily acknowledged that the presence of the ark in Ethiopia had always been deemed a sacred, holy trust—a trust for what, and until when, no one would divulge.

This possibility meshed neatly with our theory of the ark's coming forth in royal procession from Ethiopia at a prescribed time (Christ's Second Coming) to a predetermined place (the messianic temple in Jerusalem), where it would serve as the throne of Christ in the most holy place.

BEHOLD, HE IS COMING!

Let us backtrack a few centuries. Recall that when Israel returned from captivity in Babylon (between 538 and 432 B.C.), a second temple had been built in Jerusalem to restore Levitical worship to the returning Hebrews. Yet the ark and the mercy seat did not return at that time and had probably been missing for more than three hundred years.

In the absence of the ark of testimony, the focus of prophetic revelation shifted from "God dwelling in the midst of

His people" to the coming of the Messiah, heir to God's throne (Ps. 110), who would physically rule from Jerusalem (Mal. 3:1).

Malachi's prophecy came true four hundred years later as Jesus of Nazareth, the Prince of Peace, King of Kings and Lord of Lords—God's own Son—came to Jerusalem riding on a donkey, offering God's kingdom and himself as King. In the course of three short years, he spoke of ruling as King, referred to the temple as his Father's house, healed the sick, saved the lost, and performed so many miracles that if every one of them had been recorded, "even the whole world would not have room for the books that would be written" (John 21:25). By these and countless other words and deeds, Jesus demonstrated his authority to proclaim, "I and the Father are one" (John 10:30).

Yet the religious leaders of the day rejected Christ as King and delivered him to the Romans to be killed. At first glance it seems as if this extraordinary rejection had been etched in stone from before time. We tend to view it as a foregone conclusion, an event consistently foretold throughout the Old Testament. Yet within the mystery of God's omniscience and sovereignty lies God's allowance for human self-determination.

Could it be that divine provision had been made for an altogether different outcome? Could it be that God bestowed upon the residents of Jerusalem a "free choice" to *receive* Jesus as King? After all, God ultimately held that generation accountable for its rejection of Messiah, as seen in the destruction of Jerusalem in A.D. 70. That would seem to indicate that the right choice was available to them but rejected.

Without presuming to grasp how such things work, we might ask what such a scenario of acceptance could have looked like. Had that generation received Jesus as Messiah rather than crucified him, we can assume at least one thing: the ark and the mercy seat would have been available as his throne. It would have taken a procession of Ethiopian Levites only a few short weeks to travel from Axum to Jerusalem. Yet as

Passover week unfolded, at a time when Christ's own disciples fully expected to occupy places of honor in the new kingdom, it soon became clear the coronation of Jesus as King would not happen, at least not then. Christ had an appointment in Jerusalem with a cross, not a throne. Therefore, there remained no need for a throne to be brought into the temple, and therefore the ark and the mercy seat would stay hidden in Ethiopia.

Let us now imagine, if only for curiosity's sake, what might have happened if Jesus of Nazareth *had* been received and proclaimed as Messiah by Israel's religious leaders. What if he had come into his earthly kingdom and assumed his rightful place in that empty second temple? In such an event, what would Israel have done for Messiah's throne?

Here we shift the scene to Ethiopia. With a network of Falasha Jews already in place in Ethiopia, fast-traveling news of Israel's miracle-working, self-proclaimed Messiah could not have escaped the queen's attention. How would Queen Candace have likely responded to a rumor from Israel that the Messiah, the one called Jesus of Nazareth, had indeed come to his people? Besides feeling great excitement that the day had perhaps arrived to send forth the "vessels of the LORD" in royal procession, she certainly would have exercised extreme caution. Rather than sending the ark and mercy seat straightaway to Mount Zion, she would have sent a trustworthy ambassador to check out this person's credentials—and do it in a way that complied as closely as possible with the Hebrew Scriptures.

In Isaiah 52, we find a command to those "who bear the vessels of the LORD," those who are clearly *outside* the land of Israel, to "go out" and to "touch no unclean thing" along the way. That order would make the eunuch an ideal choice for such a mission, particularly if he had been entrusted with Ethiopia's treasury (including the ark and the mercy seat). Eunuchs rose to positions of high trust in those days partly because sexual sin held little temptation for them.

Such an assignment would also explain why the Ethiopian eunuch had a scroll of Isaiah in his possession. He would need a guide, or biblical profile, to cross-check Jesus' credentials. He would need to certify, beyond a shadow of doubt, that this alleged Messiah met the rigorous requirements outlined in Scripture.

After a long journey the eunuch would no doubt have arrived in Jerusalem filled with anticipation, wondering if the Chosen One already had assumed his kingdom. Had Ethiopia's day of destiny at last arrived? Yet instead of arriving to streets brimming with a royal coronation, he found Jerusalem sunk in gloom and despair. Rather than finding the King of all the earth holding court from Mount Zion, the man called Jesus had been scourged, spit upon, and crucified.

What confusion and disappointment must have ensued! For the eunuch the mission of a lifetime had ended in apparent failure. The blow must have felt crushing. Since the Pharisees had gone to such great lengths to conceal Christ's resurrection, he likely would have left Jerusalem crestfallen, shielded from the apostle's new movement, and deeply confused by the shocking turn of events.

As his chariot rolled out of Jerusalem toward Gaza, it only makes sense that he would have unsheathed the scroll one more time to review his notes and to try to understand the odd turn of events he had witnessed. And in rereading Isaiah, he would have come to chapter 52:14: "So His visage was marred more than any man, and His form more than the sons of men" (NKJV). He may have begun to wonder, *Could this possibly be what happened to Jesus of Nazareth? Could he have been the Messiah after all?*

Had he so much as entertained the thought, the next verse must have leapt off the scroll: "So shall He sprinkle many nations. Kings shall shut their mouths at Him; for what had not been told them they shall see, and what they had not heard they shall consider" (Isa. 52:15 NKJV).

Wrestling to fathom the disturbing news from Jerusalem, the eunuch may have carefully reviewed Isaiah 53 and mulled the possibility that the affliction detailed there might have foretold what would happen to Messiah. If, as the passage asserted, the King would be despised and rejected by men, with Israel's leaders shutting their mouths at him, what did that mean for the Messiah's coming reign? And what, then, of his enthronement?

It would have been about the time that Philip appeared alongside the man's chariot and asked, "Do you understand what you are reading?"

"How can I," the eunuch replied, echoing the promise of verse 15, "unless someone tells me?"

Still careful not to touch anything unclean, the eunuch invited Philip to join him in the chariot. With the scroll of Isaiah before them, the eunuch grilled Philip with questions about the identity of Messiah the King, giving Philip the opportunity to share the "good news" about Jesus. Philip's explanation confirmed Jesus' identity and messiahship, and clarified the prophecies of the returning King. Due to the blindness of that generation's leaders, the Messiah had been rejected, setting in motion a plan whereby he would return in the future, to a generation who would receive and enthrone him as King forever. Philip must have comforted the saddened eunuch with the happy truth that one can participate in God's kingdom individually by faith in Messiah, signified by water baptism.

After hearing this news, the eunuch saw a pond or lake, asked Philip to baptize him, and returned to Ethiopia, rejoicing. He would have given a succinct report to Candace: "Messiah will not establish his earthly kingdom at this time, so the ark and mercy seat are not now required. Therefore the treasures should remain in hiding in Ethiopia until the time of the King's promised return. But make no mistake, your highness: *He is coming!"*

THE FINAL PIECE OF A RIDDLE

Such a reconstructed scenario, it seemed to us, provided the final piece of a baffling riddle. And I personally felt as if I finally understood why God had chosen obscure, remote Ethiopia for the ark's secret resting place. I began to envision the arrival of that fateful day when the holy relic would emerge from the parched highlands of ancient Abyssinia, for all the world to see.

Though our conclusions and conjectures can be (and certainly will be) disputed by other biblical exegetes and godly students of the Bible, I am at least reasonably convinced that the ark and the mercy seat do indeed lie somewhere in Ethiopia. And I believe one day they will travel to Jerusalem in a royal procession following Christ's triumphal return, where the mercy seat will serve as Messiah's throne in his temple.

Part Three

IN GOD'S HANDS

Ηineteen

STORMS OVER CUSH

In April 2000, I was leading a research team across the Sinai peninsula, retracing the exodus route of Moses. Four of the team members suggested a quick trip to Ethiopia for a day visit to Axum and an excursion to see the monks on Tana Kirkos Island.

On the trip to Axum, I spoke with a monk named Haile Selassie, who made the bold claim that he could enter St. Mary of Zion church and obtain a detailed description of the object at rest there. Normally I would dismiss such a brash claim, yet Haile was the curator of the Axum Museum and had by government permission enjoyed yearly (although limited) access to St. Mary of Zion, in order to catalog the objects contained there.

I took him up on his offer and struck a handshake deal, accompanied by a modest payment, to secure his services for our research efforts. The payment made me feel uneasy and evoked an air of "payoff." But Haile soothed the awkward situation by assuring me that the monks—who had been decimated by civil wars and crushing poverty—would benefit. So it was agreed: I would return the following year and hear a description of the gold object sequestered in dark seclusion within the chapel at St. Mary of Zion.

The following day our team flew to Bahar Dar and chartered a rusty-hulled government boat to tour several islands on Lake Tana. It was to be a day excursion. As we began, the tranquil, emerald waters of Lake Tana looked as flat as a stone. It looked to be another beautiful day in the sublime spring weather of Africa.

186

We took more time than planned on Tana Kirkos, snapping photos and mingling with the monks. I then unwisely instructed our captain to pilot us to the densely jungled island of Daga Stephanos, two hours out of our way. I had intended to shoot some video of the island's royal corpses. My decision had nothing to do with the search for the ark, and I soon regretted it.

The captain had seemed skittish all day, sensing something we didn't in the lake's unpredictable temperament. With the sun about to set on Daga Stephanos, he began barking at us, quite out of character, ordering us to get back to the boat. "Hurry! Hurry!" he kept repeating, finally pulling up anchor and shouting in Amharic, "Come now, or I'm leaving without you!" That's when I finally realized he wasn't merely being difficult but had legitimate concerns for our safety. I called the rest of the team back to the dock.

An hour into our three-hour trip toward Bahar Dar, the horizon turned dark, and boiling storm clouds gathered. Foaming swells began to crash over the deck of the tug; angry whitecaps and stinging spray rocked us back and forth, despite our nervous prayers. The lake seemed big as an ocean and every bit as menacing, and I recalled the story of the Edmund Fitzgerald sinking under the waves of Lake Superior. The thought of that mighty tanker, loaded with iron ore, foundering in a November gale, made our rusty, steel-plated, smoke-spewing piece of junk seem all too vulnerable. As night rushed upon us, the wind grew violent and lashed ugly, purple-green waves over the railings, tipping the boat dangerously low to the surf.

After one particularly violent blast of spray, Misgana walked quietly over and informed me that, from his experience, the worst of the storm lay ahead.

"It will become more severe before it subsides," he said, shooting me a look that said, "You stupid American, you just *had* to get your video."

I thought humor might lighten the mood. "Maybe we'll have to swim back to shore," I joked.

Misgana didn't smile or even bat an eye. Instead he leaned back, soaking wet from the rain, elbows propped against the railing, and announced: "I will not swim to shore. I grew up on this lake. I know what lives in this water. I *know!* We would be eaten and torn to pieces by crocodiles or crushed by hippos before we reached land." Then he paused to enjoy our startled expressions and added, "If we were lucky enough to reach the shore from here, the jungle—filled with poisonous snakes and wild beasts—would kill us in an instant."

Team member Ron Hicks passed me on his way to the front of the boat. I watched as he sat down and curled his legs up, Indian style, on a small wooden bench. He'd confided to me his childhood horror of being struck by lightning, and, eyeing the crackling flashes moving toward us, he'd identified the wobbly bench as the only non-metal fixture on deck.

Thinking to break the tension, I walked over, put my left hand on his head and with my right grabbed the metal railing, then said, "So, Ron, you think you're safe from lightning on this little wooden bench?" At that instant a lightning bolt flashed in front of the bow. We both jumped a foot in the air, and I thought Ron might strangle me and throw me overboard.

187

He might have, but in that instant the boat slammed to a violent stop, seeming to rise out of the water with an ear-splitting crunch! Then, with a metal-shredding screech, we all went sprawling across the deck, bags and duffels flying about like confetti. Soon we heard the caterwaul of spinning rotors clattering against rock, followed by the panicked yelps of our poor captain screaming into his radio, cursing the storm, pleading for help, revving the engine to ever louder pitches. I picked myself off the deck and noted the expression of every face on deck turn from stunned surprise to terror.

188

Until now I hadn't taken Misgana's grim admonitions seriously. Yet suddenly the prospect of swimming for our lives seemed a distinct probability. In the inky dark waves, we'd beached the tug on a rock in the tricky narrows off the port of Bahar Dar. The captain couldn't even *see*, much less steer clear of, the rocks. Here again, I felt responsible, watching as members of our five-man crew scrambled for the only two life vests on board.

Lightning began crackling all around us. The pilot kept gunning the engine, hoping that somehow he might free us from the reef, even as the last bits of propeller blade snapped off against the rocks.

"Tell him to cut the engine!" yelled Ray Ardizonne, another team member. But it no longer mattered. The propeller shaft, sheared off at the stem, now spun free of rock or wave. Plumes of smoke belched out of the engine room as the pilot kept pumping the throttle and bellowing into his radio; then the cabin lights went out, leaving us drenched and clinging to the railing in the stinging darkness. I felt like Richard Dreyfus in the movie *Jaws*, after the great white left his trawler dead in the water in the chill of night. Thunder claps and lightning bolts exploded overhead as huge waves smashed us against the rocks, chewing up the metal hull in teeth-rattling jolts.

In the midst of the chaos, I pulled out my video camera and began taping the action: people screaming and racing around, ducking waves, and trying to gather up gear. I caught two other team members pressed against a sidewall, while Ron Hicks, still sitting Indian style on his bench, seemed to be reciting a prayer. Todd Phillips, a youth pastor from Texas, clambered over and said, "Bob, for God's sake, what do you think you're doing? *Stop taping!*"

I tried to explain. "If something really bad happens," I shouted, "I want to have at least a few really good minutes recorded for posterity." He didn't appreciate my humor.

189

Ray turned around and yelled at the others: "Let's go down below and pray!" Ray, a retired colonel in the air force, always had been a trusted friend and a steady hand in the face of danger. It was the best idea anyone had come up with, so we struggled down the steps and into the leaking cabin, where we starting praying with gusto.

"Dear Father, *help us!*" shouted Ray.

Dr. Pete Leininger chimed in: "Lord, we don't know what to do. But we trust you to get us to shore safely."

Soon we had all offered our own urgent prayers and petitions. By then the boat had tilted farther into the rocks and seemed about to break apart. Another blinding lightning bolt crashed not far away, illuminating the sky and giving us a clear view into the maw of the storm. The boat screeched across the rocks, waves pitching us so violently that I imagined the ship's metal skin splitting apart. I had begun to prepare myself for a long swim to shore when Misgana walked over and casually informed me, "The captain can't raise anyone on the radio, and we are still three and one-half miles from shore."

Yet we saw a white light flickering among the distant swells, and about fifteen minutes later an open-hulled skiff emerged from the blackness, its occupants fighting furiously against the gale. These fisherman, out for an evening catch, had somehow seen our cabin lights bobbing in the narrows. Dressed in rubber boots and rain slickers, and navigating their fragile fifteen-foot fishing craft filled with nets and floats, they finally puttered up next to our tug and told us to hop on. Their small boat strained and roiled with the wind, propelled by an antiquated, five-horsepower outboard engine. We'd been stranded on the rocks for two hours when they arrived. As we climbed aboard, the churning water came up to, and almost over, the gunwale. We reached a rickety dock on the port of Bahar Dar, waterlogged and rain-whipped yet still intact, well after midnight.

It had been a close call, one of many through the years. Ray and Pete were so thankful as they lurched up on the dock that they began pressing wads of birr into the fishermen's hands, not knowing how else to thank them. We invited our proud rescuers to join us the next morning at our hotel, where, dressed in their Sunday best, they enjoyed a lavish lunch and our endless praise. We treated them as angels of mercy and bona fide heroes, and they left us smiling, pockets bulging with our remaining birr.

A GOODWILL MISSION

Nearly a year later I would be flying back to Ethiopia with the exciting prospects of hearing from Haile Selassie. Several transatlantic calls to Haile revealed that he had indeed entered the chapel at St. Mary of Zion and had seen a golden object he believed to be the ark of the covenant. Upon my arrival, he said, he would relate to me the details of his unique experience.

We had planned to reach Addis by the morning of January 19 in order to enjoy Axum's annual two-day Timkat ceremony, held each year to exalt the ark of the covenant with parades, prayer vigils, and dancing. To help me chronicle the occasion, I had invited a small team, including my coauthor David Halbrook (just finishing up the manuscript of our second collaboration, *In Search of the Lost Mountains of Noah*), my brother Paul, and a Florida-based videographer named Brian Boorujy. Pete Leininger and his wife, Barbara, also had accepted my invitation, as had a Texas couple, Daniel and Carol Ayers.

In the row behind me slept my special guest, Mary Irwin, the wife of one of my best friends, former astronaut Jim Irwin. In a black case beneath her seat sat a black metal case holding a framed, miniature version of the Ethiopian tricolor flag. It had been specially matted next to an autographed picture of her late husband standing on the moon beside the Lunar Rover. During his 1971 *Apollo 15* moon mission, Irwin took to the lunar surface miniature flags representing every United Nations country, and over the next twenty years made a point to hand deliver each flag to its rightful homeland. It became an important part of Jim's unique missionary outreach, using the flags and his reputation to meet with heads of state from all over the planet. Since his death of a heart attack in 1991, Mary had picked up the baton. She considered our Ethiopian junket a perfect excuse not only to follow our research on the mercy seat but also to present one of the last remaining "moon flags" to Ethiopia's president, Negaso Gidada.

I found the contrast almost absurd: to think that, from my first awkward forays into Ethiopia, I would now be leading a goodwill mission to the national palace in Addis!

191

TWENTY

AXUM TIMKAT

The morning after our arrival in Ethiopia, faithful, easygoing Misgana met us at the Addis airport. He greeted our team warmly and promptly took control, walking us through the agonizingly slow ticketing process, then herding us into a small waiting area where, an hour later, we boarded a plane.

Soon we found ourselves skimming high above the parched, painted bluffs of northern Ethiopia. If all went according to plan, we'd land in Axum by 10 A.M. and drive directly to the Timkat festival.

DANCING WITH THE ARK

I heard the landing gear drop and looked out my window to watch our slow descent into craggy canyons. I took a deep breath and said a short prayer for protection—for the group, for myself—as the wheels of the plane touched down on the newly paved landing strip. The plane braked to a smooth stop, and we disembarked onto the tarmac of a relatively modern, new airport. *Where did the cow pasture go?* I wondered.

I found it amazing to learn that the government had built Axum a new airport since my last visit, little more than a year earlier. We walked inside the cozy terminal, still no bigger than a large barn, and noticed the plaster hadn't fully dried. The shiny, brushed-concrete floor and tiled walls of the luggage pickup area had a freshly grouted sheen, worlds removed from the fly-ridden shack it replaced.

"Welcome to Axum," I told the group.

Our chartered bus arrived, and the driver hastily collected our bags and drove us straight into Axum. "We must hurry," I told him, aware that the Timkat festival, underway since dawn, would be in full swing by the time we arrived.

As we sped into town, past caravans of camels and donkey traders, the members of our team stared out their windows wide-eyed, faces pressed against the glass. Having visited Axum with me the year before, Pete wore a grin, obviously excited to be back. He pointed out every detail to Barbara, who maintained a poker face, reserving judgment until she knew the full measure of hardship the stark landscape might wreak on her delicate features.

I told the driver to skip the hotel and take us directly to the main square, where, minutes later, he deposited us on the outskirts of a massive Timxat gathering. Assembled beneath the shade of a huge fig tree, the crowd, dressed uniformly in white linen, seemed to have reached a quiet interlude in the joyous proceedings. With few exceptions, every man, woman, and child wore the traditional white cotton shawls (*shemmas*) or the thicker woolen cloaks (*gebbis*). And everyone, it seemed, from church clerics to common peasants, lifted their heads to watch us step off the bus, while appearing neither distracted nor impressed. We could hear voices emanating from the center of the crowd, and I sensed we had arrived just in time. With cameras loaded and our pockets stuffed with film, we circled the crowd, working our way toward its center.

THE ENERGY BUILDS

As at the Addis-Timkat the night before, Axum's leading patriarchs, dressed in traditional white robes and black shoulder capes, leaned on tall prayer sticks and swayed to the slow, deep throb of the *kebero* (a large oval drum made of cow skin and stretched over a wood frame). A chorus of feminine voices chanted an ancient *Ge'ez* hymn; then the jingle of the silver-plated *sistra* filled the silent spaces between the *kebero*. Here and there, the deacons raised their *sistras* in unison, letting them fall with a clear, melodious jangle, like sleigh bells.

At a distance stood a group of slender, bearded priests, all robed in green silk and red skullcaps (or *k'oba*). They stood near the tree trunk, holding the Timkat festival's centerpiece and spiritual totem—a red, jewel-encrusted *tabot*—over their heads. Their vestments seemed modeled after an ancient Levite motif: costly robes bound by a gilded *k'enat* (belt), or the high priest's girdle; the tight-fitting *k'oba* (skullcap) or mitre; and the glittering *askema* (scapular). (A description of similar priestly breastplates, adorned with twelve precious stones, representing the tribes of Israel, can be found in Exodus 28.) The front of each priestly tunic also displayed a gold-stitch Axumite cross.

From the low throb and light jingle of the *kebero* and *sistra*, a quiet energy began to build. Suddenly, from its position of quiet repose, the crowd stood to its feet and began rhythmically bouncing up and down, playing an array of flutes, fiddles, lyres, and harps, one group of some thrusting ceremonial prayer sticks and *sistras* toward the sky. A cheer erupted, not unlike a war chant, then a shrill burst from the women, piercing the hot afternoon air with a sonic *"ellellellellellelle."*

At once the square shook with sound and motion, everyone poised in a heightened state of alert. From under the shade tree, surrounded by a phalanx of silk-robed patriarchs, the priest holding the *tabot* suddenly set off through the crowd, inciting an explosion of stamping feet and frenzied shouts.

With the procession pulsing and snaking toward the ruins of the St. Mary of Zion monastery, I realized we were watching—no, participating in—a dramatic reenactment of Prince Menelik's legendary journey from Jerusalem to Cush. Our team, quickly engulfed and swept along in the procession, soon scattered among troupes of dancers whirling, jumping, and shouting to the rhythms of young men pounding drums and pirouetting and praising God. At one point I caught sight of Mary, Carol, and Barbara bobbing hand-in-hand with some little girls, apparently drawn into the Timkat's hypnotic charms.

With each step the crowd seemed to swell, swallowing up spectators, small children, the elderly, lame, some obviously sick and dying, others laughing, healthy and happy, all keeping an eye on the raised *tabot,* as if the ark were leading them into battle. We meandered past the ancient walls and altars of the St. Mary of Zion monastery grounds; past the castles and fortified cathedrals; past the arched windows and stonework facades of the monastery churches; past the tall bell tower with its Arabic globes and astrological symbols; finally arriving, in a leaping, twirling, quivering mob, at the front gate of the holy chapel of the ark.

Here the crowd began to pool in waves about the iron fence, gathering energy as the lurching multitude reached a crescendo. At the front of the crowd, a young man, inflicting a savage beating on his *kebero,* led a troupe of priestly dancers leaping, shouting, and clapping their hands with otherworldly intensity. The wall of sound grew louder and louder with trumpet blasts, frenzied chanting, and the haunting thrum of dozens of ten-stringed *begegna.* Another young man, dressed in a white cotton robe, danced like a dervish before the priests, who stood marching in place, granting the pilgrims their last glimpse of the sacred *tabot*.

THE GRAND FINALE

In many respects the festival must have resembled the wild scene captured in Scripture three thousand years ago when David and all the house of Israel brought up the ark of the Lord to the gates of Jerusalem with shouting, and with the sound of the trumpet and "played before the LORD on all manner of instruments made of fir wood, even on harps, and on psalteries, and on timbrels, and on cornets, and on cymbals . . . and David danced before the LORD with all his might . . . leaping and dancing before the LORD" (2 Sam. 6:5–16 KJV).

197
Λ

The music slowly softened, and the dancers momentarily slackened; but with the crowd still chanting hymns, the priests with the *tabot* slowly circled to the back of the chapel and entered the rear gate. I skirted the crowd just in time to see them march up the stairs and into the church, disappearing inside precisely where the Atang had emerged a year earlier. The guardian never appeared—the best evidence I had seen for the *tabot's* purely ceremonial function—and the music and dancing soon abated. Yet even in silence the crowd kept swaying and praying for some time, lost in their own inner rhythms, intoxicated with praise and prepared to continue exalting God, or the ark, with their last ounce of strength. Finally, with drained and sagging countenances, the flock slowly dispersed.

It had been a stirring grand finale. Our timing had indeed been impeccable; Brian, Paul, and I captured the spectacle from every angle, causing me to feel strangely reconnected to Axum and its people.

Now that it had ended, however, and the *tabot* had retreated inside the chapel for another year, the team gathered at the bus and drove up the hill to the Yeha Hotel, where Haile stood in the lobby, waiting for me.

Twenty-one

BEHIND THE VEIL

Haile greeted me as I descended from our bus, quickly pulled me aside, and whispered, "I have seen it. I have seen the ark."

I still had no idea what Haile had witnessed. But if he had in fact seen the relic, or even a replica of it, it might be our only chance to get a detailed eyewitness account. We retired with our Ethiopian friend to the stone terrace behind the hotel restaurant and there resumed our interview.

WHAT DID IT LOOK LIKE?

More than anything I wanted a report on the wing configuration of the ark's cherubim. So on the chance that Haile really had seen something of the authentic ark and mercy seat, we had to ask, "Did its wing motif fit the image we had of a physical throne?"

"Haile," I said, "please tell us what you saw. What did the ark and the mercy seat look like?"

Without hesitating, Haile began telling us about the ark, its general size and appearance closely matching the biblical description: a wooden box, covered with gold, its shape and dimensions well within known specifications. Of course, anyone in Ethiopia could have told us as much. Haile, like every grade schooler in Axum, had known those passages from youth.

"Now, Haile," I continued, "tell us about the cherubim above the mercy seat. Exactly how are they positioned?"

With hands tracing shapes in the air, he said, "The angels had the faces of men, with their bodies stationed over the ark."

"What did the *wings* look like, Haile?"

Halbrook handed his notepad to Haile, who began sketching a rough drawing. We leaned in to watch as he drew two angels facing each other. Neither stood upright like statues, as so often depicted, but appeared as chest-high figurines, with heads bowed, facing the top of the golden box. Haile then drew wings resembling feathery arms overshadowing the ark, spread out and reverently extended, palms flat on the table. It was a rough drawing but seemed to approximate cherubim fashioned from hammered gold.

Glancing at me out of the corner of his eye, Halbrook asked, "Haile, are you sure this is what the wings looked like?"

"Yes," he said. Then without prompting he added, "As you can see, it looks as if the wings could be where someone might sit. The mercy seat is a type of chair."

INTO THE DARK

As excited as we felt to hear Haile's description of the mercy seat, our interest nevertheless shifted from the appearance of the ark to how Haile had managed to gain access to a forbidden area protected by strict security measures.

Haile attempted to tell us how he entered the chapel in the company of two monks who served as assistants to the Atang. They had entered under the official guise of cataloging some of the thousands of history books, crosses, crowns, paintings, and manuscripts stored in the chapel's basement.

The tone of Haile's voice grew dark as he explained how he and the two monks left the storage chamber and walked slowly upstairs, through several heavily reinforced wooden doors, until they reached the outer chamber of the inner sanctum. With words vague and imprecise, and spoken so softly we could barely hear them, Haile said they had entered into the most holy place, where, in the shadows, they saw a large stone chamber sitting atop a stone pedestal, like a mausoleum vault, approximately five feet long and four feet high. The top of the structure was gabled, like the roof of a house.

201

"Where was the guardian?" Halbrook asked. "Isn't he the only one who ever sees the holy relic? How did you and these monks manage to get past the guardian into the inner sanctum?"

The question seemed no different from asking a common Levite in Solomon's day how he had managed to penetrate the Holy of Holies. He *couldn't* have. Haile's story seemed to make no sense in a culture that revered the ark with an ardor every bit as zealous as their ancient Hebrew brethren. Yet Haile recounted each step with almost mechanical detail.

"Haile," Halbrook continued, "where was the guardian of the ark when you and the monks entered the inner sanctuary?"

Haile bowed his head. "The guardian stood in the next room."

"In the next room?" I asked. "Is that allowed? Are you allowed to do this?"

"Yes, we are allowed," he nodded, "because of my appointment as government official of the museum."

"OK, Haile," I sighed, "once you entered the inner sanctuary, what did you do? What happened?"

"It was very dark," he replied. "One of the monks and I walked over and began to open up the stone vault housing the ark. It was heavy, hard to move. Once we slid it from its position, we noticed that there was a silver box inside, an ornate inner lining that surrounded and protected the ark."

Haile now spoke in a whisper. "As the monk opened the doors of the box that contains the ark, a bright reflection, like gold, came out." He shook his head back and forth, the image still haunting him. "I remember it like a dream. Yes, it seemed like a dream."

Several moments passed before he added, "We must have fallen down, for when I opened my eyes, we all lay on the floor. We lay there, unable to move; I don't know for how long. They had to pull us out. They took us to a hospital." His eyes grew large. "After four days I was taken from the hospital and placed in jail, under arrest, the authorities screaming at me, demanding to know, 'Who told you to register the ark?' I told them, 'Narud. Narud gave us permission.' They finally released me."

I recognized Narud's name as the monastery patriarch I had interviewed two years earlier. He waved a hand across his face. "It was bad, and now my eyes have been damaged. I have trouble seeing."

"What happened to the other monks?" I asked.

"Three weeks ago," he said with a heavy breath, "one of the monks died from injuries he sustained inside the chapel. Tomorrow, if you like, we will visit his grave."

(The next day I did visit the monk's grave. There I met the brother of the deceased monk, who told me the story exactly as Haile had described it.)

"What about the other monk?" Halbrook asked.

"He is sick and can no longer continue his work at the chapel. He has been forced to retire. He can barely stand. It seems his body is dying."

(I also interviewed this second monk. He was old and related the same story Haile had told. Two days after our interview, he also died.)

Halbrook then asked Haile about his eyes. "Tell us exactly how that happened," he said.

Haile rubbed his eyes, then stared at his open palms. "It was from looking at the ark. When I awoke on the floor of the chapel, my eyes hurt, and they hurt still. They have been this way since that day."

A CHILLING TURN

The search for the ark had taken a chilling turn, and we found ourselves treading a path toward the surreal. If Haile told the truth, *something* had happened inside the chapel.

Had they actually seen the genuine ark? Or had the thought of the ark's awesome power, magnified by a lifetime of potent religious indoctrination, overwhelmed their guilty consciences? Perhaps the idea of the ark's holy and unapproachable stature struck such fear in their hearts that they fell back, as if slain, at the first glint of a metallic reflection.

Though we already knew that an object of some distinction sat inside the chapel, Haile could not seem to put his experience into words. Whatever they saw—a tangible object or a hallucination—it had inflicted a devastating toll.

For long moments we sat there on the breezy terrace, saying nothing. Haile finally broke the silence. "I must go now," he said and rose to leave.

I saw no point in pressing the interrogation. Haile seemed too shaken, and my own thoughts had become muddled. Halbrook nodded, and we both escorted Haile down to the lobby.

"Good night, Haile," we said. Without turning or even bothering to reply, Haile slowly walked down the road and vanished into the night.

203

Twenty-two

A FINAL LOOK AROUND

With our business in Axum finished, we boarded an Ethiopian Airlines turboprop bound for Gondar, located fifty miles north of Lake Tana and long recognized as the Camelot of Africa.

I hoped to complete an important leg of our research by visiting one of a handful of the remaining Falasha villages scattered at the edge of the Simien Mountains. I had long wanted to meet the Falashas, owing primarily to their probable connections to ancient Israel.

THE BATHING PALACE

Before visiting the Falashas, however, we toured the famous Bathing Palace, so named for its rectangular, neatly walled man-made lake. The lake is filled with water once a year for Timkat.

Inspecting the moss green lake, I imagined the recent horde of celebrants prancing wildly about the lake, chanting and praying under a Gondarine sunset as priests paraded the sacred *tabotat* about the perimeter. Enormous crowds come to this bathing place each year during Timkat, thousands of them camping overnight on the grassy lawns surrounding the courtyard. With the first rays of dawn, they rouse themselves, filling the compound with flailing leaps and pirouettes. Then, at the climactic moment, the people begin throwing themselves into the lake—some fully clothed, some naked—in a rapturous, mass baptismal rite.

I imagined the church's staid priests marching back and forth to deafening cheers as they balanced the velvet-wrapped *tabotat* on their heads, the sounds of tambourines, cymbals, and trumpet blasts everywhere. The ecstatic, soaking-wet procession would slowly circumnavigate the lake until the priests disappeared into the church for another year, restoring the *tabotat* to its resting place behind the veil of the Holy of Holies.

As I sat against the courtyard wall, it struck me that these revelries were what I loved so about Ethiopia. They connected me spiritually to something I'd been searching for—an unbridled fervor for the things of God. Maybe it suggested to me what the early church must have been: a deeply committed group of radical disciples, in love with Jesus and extreme in their faith. Those first apostles, aflame with the fire of God, caused a stir everywhere they went. Unashamed of the gospel and unabashed in their worship, they changed their world forever. Western Christians like myself could hardly comprehend them, conditioned as we have become to sitting quietly in church as a pastor preaches his Sunday message.

To the contrary, these Ethiopian Christians erupt once a year into a jubilant, almost ferocious worship of God. This raw, earthy form of devotion struck me as a liberated expression of awe for an omnipotent, holy God. If I never returned to Ethiopia, it would be her people's uncontrolled, childlike adoration of God that I would miss the most.

THE PLIGHT OF THE FALASHAS

The Falashas of northern Ethiopia stand a world apart from their Christian neighbors. The pronounced Old Testament character of the Falashas' religion suggests that their ancestors arrived in Ethiopia at an early date, perhaps as early as 500 B.C. Their archaic religious practices lead some scholars to conclude that these "black Jews" separated from mainstream Judaism well before 200 B.C., when the Talmud and many modern Jewish feasts came into being. Since the Falashas neither observe nor recognize feasts such as Hanukkah (Feast of Dedication of the Temple, instituted in 164 B.C.), or the Feast of Purim (firmly in place by 425 B.C.), we have strong reason to think they became isolated from the body of world Judaism well before 425 B.C.[1]

Moreover, their ignorance of either the Babylonian or the Jerusalem Talmud (both of which were composed during and after the time of the Babylonian captivity[2]), combined with a strict conformance to the teachings of the Torah, leaves the Falashas as perhaps the only remaining practitioners of pure Hebrew "fundamentalism." Not only do they afford great respect and obedience to the Pentateuch (the first five books of the Bible), they maintain a rigid adherence to food restrictions detailed in Leviticus and Deuteronomy.[3] Both traits distinguish the Falashas as ardent followers of a brand of Hebrew religion that would have been widespread among Israel's twelve tribes during Solomon's reign. It is also worth noting that, if the Falashas indeed acquired their faith before 425 B.C., the possibility exists that their ancestors arrived in Ethiopia at a time roughly equal to the ark's disappearance from the temple in Jerusalem.[4]

Until recently the Falashas practiced something that modern Jews abandoned nearly two thousand years ago: ritualistic animal sacrifice. This hallmark Old Testament rite, unseen anywhere else in the world, dates the Falashas to a time prior to the radical reforms instituted by King Josiah in the wake of Manasseh's apostasy.

Today the Falashas are in decline. From a population of nearly 500,000 in 1600, their numbers dropped to 150,000 by the late nineteenth century; by the first quarter of the twentieth-century, the figure had plummeted to just 50,000; and sixty years later, during the famine of 1984, the Falasha population of Ethiopia dropped to a mere 28,000.[5]

The past three decades had seen a massive exodus of Falashas to Israel, prompted by a 1973 ruling by Israel's chief rabbis which officially recognized the Falashas as "true Jews" and rendered them eligible for Israeli citizenship under terms of the Law of Return.[6] Ironically, though the Falashas had been widely recognized as "true Jews" since the early nineteenth century, it was their archaic brand of faith that for years stalled their quest to win Israeli citizenship. Because of their Torah-based social and religious behavior, Israel's rabbinical delegation refused to recognize them. To twentieth-century Jews, the Falashas' ignorance of modern Talmudic precepts, coupled with their radical "fundamentalism,"[7] made them seem like some bizarre sect.

And while the 1973 ruling offered hope to tens of thousands of yearning Falashas, it proved to be, in reality, a bureaucratic bottleneck, stifling large-scale immigration. Governmental foot-dragging, endless paperwork, and muddled communication left tens of thousands of Falashas stranded in Ethiopia while thousands more flooded illegally into refugee camps in Sudan, where they hoped to be airlifted to Israel. From just such a refugee camp in 1984, an emergency airlift known as Operation Moses rescued twelve thousand starving Falashas.

In 1989, however, the floodgates burst open anew when Addis Ababa, after a sixteen-year break, formally restored diplomatic relations with Jerusalem, securing a pledge to allow *all* Falashas to emigrate to Israel. By then, only about fifteen thousand Falashas remained. By the 1990s, Falasha numbers in northern Ethiopia had dwindled fast, and today, in a handful of villages like Weleka, they can probably be counted in the hundreds.

ON TO WELEKA VILLAGE

Our journey to Weleka Village took us a little more than twenty minutes into the foothills north of Gondar. Our van trundled up a rutted mountain road into a dense patch of wooded hills and deposited us at the village's drab front gate.

Misgana rushed into the village to arrange for a host. We waited for him beside the van, noting several unmistakably Hebrew emblems inside the gate, including a bronze Star of David perched atop a hut and a large block of stone in the shape of a lion—the lion of Judah—whitewashed with the words, "Welcome to Weleka."

Misgana soon returned, joined by a pleasant-looking woman encircled by a gaggle of children. He introduced her as Marye, the village's surrogate mom. She looked to be in her early forties and wore a loose, gray-check dress frayed around the seams. She had wrapped a white prayer shawl twice around her waist, and a gold medallion emblazoned with the Star of David hung from a chain on her neck. Despite our impromptu arrival, she seemed happy to see us.

With natural ease and grace she ushered us up the hill to her mud thatch hut. We all crowded inside, hardly knowing what to expect, while she motioned for us to sit on a rough assortment of wooden benches and wicker chairs.

With Misgana narrating her every movement, Marye squatted silently on a footstool and began stoking a small metal brazier, fanning the red buttons of coals in preparation for what Misgana described as a traditional Ethiopian coffee ceremony. At once, a pungent, pleasant smell of incense filled the hutch.

Sensing we had landed in good hands, we settled back in our chairs, content to relax and watch.

Marye spread freshly cut sprigs of grass on a tray that held eleven small finger cups, then scattered grass on the floor near our feet to cleanse and freshen the room for her guests. By now we all knew of Ethiopia's love affair with coffee and had each enjoyed countless strong, savory cups.

With her warm smile and tranquil manner, Marye made us feel like honored guests. From a darkened corner she produced a long-handled pan, in which she placed a handful of green coffee beans; holding it over the brazier, she shook it gently, roasting the beans until they achieved a dark chocolate hue. A trickle of smoke rose from the now-sizzling beans, filling the hutch with a sharp, spicy odor. Marye passed the pan around, motioning for us to inhale the rich aroma. Then she placed the beans in a stone mortar and, using a section of iron rebar, pounded them to a fine powder; then she scooped the coffee into a traditional clay pot for brewing.

While the coffee steeped, Marye busied herself with an elaborate cup-washing ritual, swishing steaming water into each cup and meticulously scrubbing them—not once but three times. I had participated in Ethiopian coffee ceremonies before, but never had I witnessed such a thorough washing—a nod, no doubt, to Hebrew laws of cleanliness. When she at last poured us our first steaming cups of espresso, we were practically foaming at the mouth.

As I leaned back in my chair, I could see a special bond forming between Mary Irwin and Marye. Mary had made a special effort to help Marye at each stage of the ceremony, fanning the coals as our host attended to the coffee beans. In the midst of swirling smoke from incense and burning coals, it seemed a strange and wonderful phenomenon—two different women from unfamiliar worlds, connecting so quickly on some unspoken wavelength.

The afternoon passed like a warm, summer breeze. In due time Halbrook and I began to interview Marye, with Misgana translating.

"Do you speak Hebrew?" Halbrook asked.

"I speak a little Hebrew," she smiled. "I *pray* in Hebrew. I light the Shabbat candles at sundown and pray."

"How many live in Weleka village?"

"Not long ago we had three hundred and fifty families, but most have gone to Israel. Now we have only a few dozen."

"Where is your family?"

Here, sadness slowly dissolved her smile. "I am the only one left," she said. "My sister and mother died in the desert of Sudan, trying to reach Israel. They traveled mostly at night, but they had to cross a part of the Sahara Desert. They were part of a large group, maybe two hundred, mostly young people." She paused, took a deep breath, and tried to muster some cheer. "They died with a happy dream to be in Israel."

"How did they die?"

"Of hunger. There was not enough to drink or eat in the refugee camp."

"What about your father?"

"My father and three brothers died in the war with Eritrea."

"Do you have a husband?"

"I lost my husband in the war also."

"Did *all* your men fight in the war?"

"Yes, the Jewish people were forced to join under the Mengistu regime. Many of our men died."

"Marye," Halbrook said, "when we arrived in your village, we noticed many children and some women. Where are all the men?"

"All of the men have gone to Israel," she said, eyes lowered. "They have all gone."

"Why did the men leave the women and children behind?"

She fidgeted on her stool. "They were approved by the government to leave, so they left." She shrugged. "We cannot blame them. The rest of us are trying to go, too."

"How do you survive, now that the men are gone?"

"We survive," she said, pointing to a bench outside the door, "by making pots of clay and selling them."

"Will you soon be able to go to Israel and join the others?" I asked.

"We are all trying, all of the women and children." Then she explained how many things must fall into place for a Falasha to leave Ethiopia. For one, each must have a sponsor from Israel. "I have been fortunate to have acquired such a sponsor," she said, smiling. "It allowed me to take a trip to Addis Ababa to undergo blood tests, to prove my Jewish roots. We must be able to trace our Hebrew roots back several generations. The chief from our village vouched for me, so I was allowed to go to Addis for my interview. Now I am just waiting for all the paperwork to be completed."

"How long must you wait to find out?"

She stared out the door of the hut and, with a trace of resignation, said, "I don't know. I have been waiting a long time. Each of us must pay our own way. It is expensive. I will need a sponsor for that, too." Then she grinned shyly and lifted her eyes as if recalling a childhood dream. "Oh, I cannot wait to be in Israel! It is the home of my roots, of my people, of our original land. One of my uncles now lives in Tel Aviv." Another deep sigh. "I would give anything to see the people I knew as a child, all those who now live in Israel."

"Are you in communication with your relatives in Israel?"

"No, there is no way to communicate; though, if I had to, I could probably contact them through the Ethiopian Embassy in Addis."

In time the conversation eased toward the ark of the covenant. We asked if she believed the biblical ark rested in Axum.

"Most certainly!" she replied, pressing a hand to her heart. "The ark of the covenant was given to Moses to help the Israelites follow the Ten Commandments. Menelik brought it to Ethiopia, where it was taken away from the Jews by the Christians. One day it will be brought back to Israel . . . when the timing is right."

As the sun ripened and began to set in the bowl of the Simien Mountains, we said our thanks and prepared to leave. As we rose to leave, I noticed Marye's lip begin to quiver; when we asked what was wrong, she squinted her eyes, wrinkled her nose, and began to cry like a little girl about to be torn from her family. Mary Irwin rushed over to embrace her.

"Tell us why are you crying, Marye," she said.

With trembling voice, Marye replied, "It makes me sad to see you go. For one afternoon, at least, it felt like I had a family again. I know you cannot, but I wish you could stay."

In that instant we all surrounded Marye, enveloping her with hugs, trying to comfort her. Seeing Marye's tears and feeling our own pain at parting, we knew a connection had occurred, knitting our hearts on a level we couldn't fully understand.

Struggling to say good-bye, we shed more tears and gave more hugs. Finally we returned to the van, then waved a sad good-bye. As we drove down the hill toward Gondar, Halbrook came up to sit next to me, Bible in hand. He thumbed through several pages before speaking, then said, "Bob, I was just curious—did it seem strange to you that all the men had gone, leaving only women and children behind?"

I nodded. "Yes, it did seem strange—men leaving their families behind. Why do you ask?"

213

Still flipping pages, he said, "I don't mean, simply, that the men left their families, but what about the *women* left behind?"

"What do you mean?"

Turning a page, he said, "Well, for some reason, sitting in Marye's hutch, hearing her talk about herself and a few woman being the only adults left in the village, I couldn't stop thinking . . ."

"About what?"

"About that passage in Zephaniah. You know, the verse prophesying about the gift being brought out of Ethiopia." He paused. "Do you remember what the *end* of that verse says?"

"No, tell me."

Marking the passage with his finger, he began to read slowly: "From beyond the rivers of Ethiopia My worshipers, the *daughter* of My dispersed ones, shall bring My offering" (Zeph. 3:10 NKJV). Then he looked up. Scratching his head, he said, "For some reason, sitting with Marye, that verse popped into my mind. Did it ever occur to you that, just maybe, the Falashas are the 'dispersed ones' spoken of in that passage, and that Marye or one of these other women might be the 'daughter' of the dispersed ones, who will bring the offering up from Ethiopia?"

The comment jolted me. I grabbed the Bible and read the verse for myself. I'd read it dozens of times, but it never connected—at least, not like this. Halbrook started to chuckle.

"Wouldn't it be wild," he said, "if Marye and the rest of those abandoned women were the ones God chose, from before time, to lead a royal procession from Axum, bearing the ark? Can you imagine it, Bob, these 'daughters' of the Falasha Jews bearing the ark into the messianic temple in Jerusalem, after the Second Coming?"

The thought seemed absurd. Who could ever prove it? Yet, having met the beautiful, gentle-spirited Marye, it suddenly struck me as not so absurd.

Isn't that how God usually works, using the meekest of the meek to humble the proud, appointing the lowly and simple to carry out his most sublime plans? In God's unpredictable economy, Marye and her kin—humblest of the humble of the poor, destitute Falasha Jews—might well be the perfect choice to lead Messiah's royal procession.

Without expecting it our trip had reached a climax. A simple afternoon at Weleka Village had capped my personal quest for the ark. As we entered our journey's final leg, I knew I had only one duty left to perform in Ethiopia.

Twenty-three

THE KING ON HIS THRONE

Two long, maroon Mercedes sedans, sent by the Ethiopian National Palace, arrived at the Sheraton Addis early Saturday to retrieve us. On this morning of our last full day in Ethiopia, Mary Irwin and our team had been invited to present President Negaso Gidada a framed Ethiopian tricolor flag, the one that had traveled with her husband to the moon.

Through dozens of phone calls from hotel lobbies across Ethiopia's northern highlands, we had finally arranged an audience with the president. Only the day before his office had graciously invited our entire team to the palace for the ceremony. The press would be on hand as well to record the president's historic exchange with the wife of the famous American astronaut.

Negaso's personal chauffeurs picked us up and drove us twenty minutes across town, slowing down as we approached the faded gray-marble pillars and iron-spiked gates guarding the entrance to the National Palace. Three armed guards in camouflage fatigues waved us in; we proceeded down a narrow, tree-lined lane, through stunning gardens and lush lawns, easing to a stop in front of a huge white building—very much a presidential palace, replete with towering ivory pillars and delicate religious statuary.

A broad flight of polished marble steps led to a huge, recessed entryway, above which we noticed a series of bas relief panels adorned with sculpted images of warrior kings and angels. Off to a side, standing sentry, stood a ten-foot tall statue of a young David, staff in hand, poised over a kneeling ram. On either side of the entryway blossomed burgundy bougainvillea and clusters of closely manicured palms. In front of the palace lay a charming garden maze bounded by a spacious, jade lawn.

218

A red carpet trailed down the palace steps to the sedans. We stepped out and followed it up into the palace, where butlers in double-breasted suits escorted us inside the foyer, carpeted all in red and dominated by an enormous tiger-skin rug, mouth agape. By any measure this engagement constituted a fitting conclusion to our Ethiopian adventure.

THE MISSION

As if in a pipe dream, we found ourselves stepping from luxury sedans to meet with the supreme ruler of Ethiopia at the National Palace. A team of butlers ushered us from the elegant foyer into a luxurious receiving room, just right of the main entryway.

Despite the extravagant trappings, our team struck a distinguished pose. Seated primly around a round, polished mahogany table bedecked with delicate Ethiopian artworks—Red Sea seashells, native pottery, and traditional wood carvings—our men wore suits and ties, while the women struck a classic pose in fine evening wear.

I almost laughed. The pomp and ceremony, the chauffeurs and butlers, the gardens and lavish presidential trappings seemed an absurd contrast to my first visit to Ethiopia. Back then, wandering the streets with Joby Book, we could barely catch a cab from the airport, then found ourselves holed up at an inner-city fleabag with cockroaches the size of my boot. It would have seemed fantasy to imagine that, one day, I'd lead a chauffeured U.S. delegation to these stately offices.

As this trip had unfolded, however, I had moved toward a larger view of events and had come to regard this meeting as a divine appointment. As I sat in my silk-embroidered, wingback chair, I rehearsed what I had only recently perceived as my part in the day's ceremony. I'd been praying about it since Axum and now felt certain what I must do.

During the course of Mary's presentation, I had decided, I would attempt to offer the president our interpretation of Isaiah 18. I would try to explain how the ark of the covenant and the mercy seat might one day emerge from Ethiopia to serve as the literal throne of the returning Messiah.

With everything I had seen and experienced these past weeks, I now felt a burden to make known to the Ethiopian leadership what we had uncovered in Scripture. If our theory were true, they deserved to know about it.

THE MIRACLE OF ISRAEL

What would the president think of our theory? How would he respond? Would he prove to be a staunch advocate of his country's ancient ark traditions or show himself to be an intellectual sophisticate, merely tolerating the legends and superstitions of his lowbrow countrymen?

And even if he did hold to the Axum tradition, how would he receive news of Messiah's throne, much less the concept of a rebuilt temple in Jerusalem? The latter topic, I knew, seemed a certifiable impossibility to most of the world. The uneasy state of global affairs would make any mention of a third temple in Jerusalem sound inflammatory.

Yet, taking a step back and weighing events from a larger perspective, far stranger things have happened. Take, for

219

instance, the existence—two thousand years after Titus destroyed the second temple in A.D. 70, razed Jerusalem, and sent Jews scattering to the ends of the earth—of the modern state of Israel. For nearly twenty centuries it seemed unthinkable that Israel, Jerusalem, the Jews, or the Temple Mount could ever again hope to play any role in human history. Jesus himself warned the disciples that Herod's temple and the city of Jerusalem would be utterly destroyed by the Romans, obliterating not only the temple but also the concept of "Israel" as it was once known.

220

Over the next two centuries, as the Romans dispersed the Jews throughout the civilized world and the church lost sight of her Jewish roots, theologians and thinkers alike began to presume that God was finished with Israel forever. How could God fulfill promises to a nation that no longer existed? How could he make his triumphant return to a dispersed people with nothing more than an ethnic label to identify them? And how could the returning Messiah rule physically from a temple that had long since been erased from the face of the earth?

The hard evidence of history seemed to have painted Israel out of the picture. Christians everywhere, weighing the known "facts," began to exchange belief in a physical, literal fulfillment of prophecy for a symbolic, allegorical unfolding of events. Rather than daring to imagine a literal fulfillment of all God promised in his covenant with Abraham and subsequent prophecies to the Hebrews, religious thinkers began seeing these promises in metaphorical terms. Israel, Jerusalem, and the temple began to be perceived as mere pictures of the church, Christians, and Christ's rule in believing hearts.

It seemed only natural, even reasonable, that God's promises should not be taken literally. How could they refer to actual events that, from every shred of evidence, seemed impossible? Israel would never again exist; the Jews—if they survived the countless persecutions leveled against them—

would never again possess the land of Palestine; and the Temple Mount would never be anything more than the site of two Islamic structures.

Reflecting on it all in the anteroom of the presidential palace, I found myself baffled anew at the implausible chronology of events. For if anything was more unlikely than God's preservation of the ark and the mercy seat in Ethiopia, it had to be the threefold phenomenon of the regathering of Jews to their historic homeland, the rebirth of Israel, and the reemergence of Jerusalem and its Temple Mount as the epicenter of human events.

The unpredictability of this dumbfounding convergence should cause any reasonable person to ask, "How could this be?" Who could have predicted that on November 30, 1947, the general assembly of the United Nations would approve a plan to divide British-administered Palestine into an Arab state and a Jewish state? And who could have forecast that, despite Arab military efforts, David Ben Gurion would stand in a Tel Aviv museum on May 14, 1948, and declare the birth of the modern state of Israel?

And yet today Israel dominates the news. Scarcely a day goes by without a bulletin of some new cultural clash, terrorist tragedy, or political uprising rocking Israel. From the economic linchpin of Arab oil reserves to the perpetual threat of global terrorism, all eyes have turned toward Israel and the Jews.

EXACTLY WHAT THE BIBLE FORETOLD LONG AGO!

Defying every law of probability, the Bible is making good on a prophecy more than fifteen hundred years old: that the Jews would return to their homeland and become once more a sovereign nation. Everything we have seen to date has played out exactly as God's Word predicted; not allegorically, but literally; not figuratively, but physically. In the face of the longest odds imaginable, God's Word has once more proved itself true.

This same Bible also gives us advance notice of Messiah's climactic and victorious return, and, apparently, his enthronement in the Holy of Holies in the rebuilt Jerusalem temple. How this anticipated scenario will play out in the days and years to come, only God knows. But for now—for us—the focus had shifted back to Ethiopia. How would our findings, and how would this meeting, fit into the grander scheme?

222

THE MESSAGE

A palace steward appeared in the doorway, asked us to rise, then led us across the vestibule into a large, beautifully appointed presidential reception hall. The breathtaking room, adorned with Persian rugs the size of dance floors, gold-trimmed frescoes, silk tapestries, and multitiered crystal chandeliers that cast feathery circles of light on the floor, had survived a staggering succession of wars, coups, revolutions, and uprisings.

At the back of the room stood the president and his attendants; behind them, in a half-circle, sat a large, gold-paneled divider inlaid with portraits of past emperors, girded at either end by elephant tusks the size of tall men. Mary Irwin stood forward, cradling the framed Ethiopian flag carefully in her arms. It had been tastefully matted with an autographed picture of her husband standing on the moon, beside the lunar module. Brian stood off in a corner, rolling video. The rest of us formed a tight line behind Mary.

President Negaso, a diminutive, bespectacled fellow with warm eyes and a light, upturned mustache, watched us from the back of the room. We approached slowly, but he waved us forward, eager to shake each of our hands and learn our names. After hurried greetings his senior assistant lined us up for the formal presentation. Mary moved lightly toward the president, who was dressed nattily in a dark suit and red tie. Speaking slowly, with a low, measured voice, she gracefully informed him that the Ethiopian flag she carried, emblazoned with the lion of Judah, had been with her husband on the surface of the moon for three days and should now be regarded as a gift of peace and brotherhood from the American people.

"We come from America in peace and Christian love," she said, extending the frame toward the president. "On behalf of my late husband, we present you this gift with great affection from the people of the United States of America."

Seconds before her presentation, Mary had sliced her hand on an edge of the picture frame, and now she shook hands with the president with a blood-splotched tissue pressed into her palm. No one seemed to notice or care; the president received the gift as a "highly esteemed national treasure," and formally ended the presentation by handing each of us a leather-bound copy of the Ethiopian constitution. Within moments butlers and maids passed out drinks and hors d'oeuvres on silver trays, and everyone began shaking hands and mingling.

Seeing our opportunity, Halbrook and I walked forward and stood beside the president. He caught our eye and greeted us warmly, appearing keen and alert to hear whatever we had to say. His first words praised Mary's short speech; he happily explained how his father had been a Presbyterian minister and one of the first in Ethiopia to learn Braille.

"I myself became a Christian when missionaries from Pennsylvania came over and witnessed to my father," he said proudly. "He got saved, and the rest of us followed suit."

"Ah," I said, "it is good to know we share a noble Savior." Aware our time was short, I politely interjected: "Mr. President, my name is Bob Cornuke. I have spent the past seven years researching the ark of the covenant in Axum. In that time I have grown to love the people of your country and have been repeatedly blessed by their friendship and hospitality."

At the mention of the ark, the president's eyes lit up.

"Ah," he said, "have you had the opportunity to meet the guardian of the ark?"

"Yes sir," I replied. "I have met with the guardian twice, the second time on this trip." I took a breath, and, praying my words would be well received, added, "Mr. President, forgive me for being so bold, but may I ask, do *you* believe the ark lies in Axum?"

He nodded and smiled. "I *know* it is," he said, before checking himself. "Or, should I say, as President of Ethiopia, I *believe* it is."

Good, I thought, *he believes in the ark.*

"Then you might be interested," I continued, "to know what the Bible—particularly the prophet Isaiah—has to say about the ark's purpose for residing in Ethiopia?"

"Yes, of course," Negaso said with a slight grin and a bow. "I have read Isaiah, but I have never been sure how to understand it. What is your interpretation?"

How interesting, I thought: *like the Ethiopian eunuch in Philip's day, the current president of Ethiopia also struggles with Isaiah's prose.* By the eager inflection in his voice, I reckoned him a student of the Bible.

"Well, Mr. President," I pressed on, "I believe Isaiah 18 speaks directly of a 'great gift' being brought out of Ethiopia."

The president looked me squarely in the eye. "And what gift would *that* be?"

I quickly ran down our research, and then, without elaborating, declared, "Our research suggests that the ark of the covenant and the top of the ark, known as the mercy seat, is the 'offering' that will be brought out of Ethiopia one day, to serve as the throne of the returning Messiah, Jesus Christ."

The president's expression remained circumspect. "Mr. Cornuke, is it?" he replied. "Please, allow me to clarify. You are saying that, from your research, you believe the ark will come out of Ethiopia to one day serve as the Savior's *throne?*"

I smiled. "Yes, Mr. President. Biblical prophecy tells us that on the day of the Lord, or the Second Coming, a third temple will already have been built in Jerusalem. This temple is described in Ezekiel 43 as the place where Messiah's throne will be." I paused. "The picture clearly suggests that this prophecy will be fulfilled in the person of Messiah, God in human flesh, sitting, ruling, reigning, and speaking his will from the mercy seat—his throne in the messianic temple."

I waited for the words to sink in, then concluded: "Mr. President, from all we have learned, we believe that this great gift, Messiah's throne, will come from Cush, or Ethiopia. And we believe it may be the mercy seat of the ark that Ethiopia now possesses."

He stood face-to-face with Halbrook and me, weighing these words. He seemed speechless, and for a moment I feared that I had overstepped my bounds. At last he extended his hand and in the warmest, gentlest manner said, "Thank you, *sincerely,* for sharing this with me. I have not heard such a thing before, but it is something, I assure you, I will take into consideration as we determine how best to protect the holy ark."

Halbrook and I bowed.

"We are honored to have had this opportunity, Mr. President," I said. "As one who understands the significance of Ethiopia in these trying times, I earnestly encourage you and your successors to do everything within your powers to protect zealously the ark that you say is in your country's care."

He smiled, thanked us again, turned, and, glancing back, bid our party a warm farewell. His minister of culture stepped forward and ushered us back out to the front entrance. A crowd of local media had gathered on the steps to interview Mary. I checked my watch; could it be possible that our entire time in the palace had lasted only thirty minutes? I waited beside the sedan, relieved and exhilarated, feeling somehow unburdened, even satisfied, that I had finished what I came to do. I felt my work in Ethiopia now complete.

THE END OF THE MATTER

Had the president thought me crazy? It did not seem so, for his eyes had flashed instant enthusiasm, perhaps even recognition, at my suggestion. The theory seemed to register, perhaps, with something he had been deliberating. I could see it in his eyes—he *knew*, too.

226

We returned to the sedans for the drive back to our hotel. Somehow I couldn't shake my excitement.

Oh, Ethiopia!

What a country. What a people. What a culture. Plagued with unspeakable poverty yet overflowing with the richness of human kindness, Ethiopia had lodged itself in my heart as the most mysterious land I would ever visited, concealing secrets I would never understand if I lived among these people one hundred years.

The end of the matter is simply this: if what lies in Axum is the true ark, then God's protective hand is upon it. It will not be moved, seen, or touched before its time. God will do what God will do, directing events for his own pleasure, at his own discretion, to his own ends—sometimes in cooperation with, but usually in spite of, what humans think or do.

And what of my Ethiopian adventures? Have I indeed brushed close to the most holy object in history? I believe so, though my role or involvement in it no longer seems to matter. I have visited a land shadowed with buzzing wings, have come to know its smooth-skinned people, and in their stirring company I have been transformed.

One day, I believe, when Messiah's banner is raised on the mountains of Israel and when his trumpet sounds, God's holy offering will rise from this nation of strange speech, from this land divided by rivers—from Ethiopia. At that time a gift will be brought to Mount Zion, to the place of the name of the Lord of hosts.

I also believe that I, along with all believers in Jesus the Messiah, will see that day as we follow him in his return, conquest, and triumphal entry into Jerusalem. But until then, even if I never return to this fabled land, I could not now, or ever, hope to see more than my Lord already has revealed through his precious Word:

> Your procession has come into view, O God,
> the procession of my God and King into the sanctuary.
> In front are the singers, after them the musicians;
> with them are the maidens playing tambourines.
> Praise God in the great congregation;
> praise the LORD in the assembly of Israel.
> There is the little tribe of Benjamin, leading them,
> there the great throng of Judah's princes,
> and there the princes of Zebulun and of Naphtali.
> Summon your power, O God;
> show us your strength, O God, as you have done before.
> Because of your temple at Jerusalem
> kings will bring you gifts.
> Rebuke the beast among the reeds,
> the herd of bulls among the calves of the nations.
> Humbled, may it bring bars of silver.
> Scatter the nations who delight in war.
> Envoys will come from Egypt;
> Cush will submit herself to God.
> Sing to God, O kingdoms of the earth,
> sing praise to the Lord (Ps. 68:24–32).

Notes

Chapter 1

1. William H. Honan, "Robert Van Kampen, Investor and Bible Collector, Dies at 60," *The New York Times*, 4 November 1999, obituaries.

Chapter 2

1. *Jerusalem Bible* (London: Eyre & Spottiswoode, 1968), Chronological Table, 346.

2. *Hebrew-English Edition of the Babylonian Talmud* (New York: Soncino Press, 1974), 53b.

3. Zev Vilnay, *Legends of Jerusalem: The Sacred Land*, vol. 1 (Philadelphia: Jewish Publication Society of America, 1973), 123.

4. 2 Maccabees 2:1.

5. Herbert Danby, trans., *The Mishnah* (Oxford: University Press, 1989), 158.

6. Randall Price, *In Search of Temple Treasures: The Lost Ark and the Last Days* (Eugene, Oreg.: Harvest House Publishers, 1994), 98.

7. Ibid., 100.

8. Ibid., 118.

9. Neil Asher Silberman, *Digging for God and Country: Exploration, Archaeology and the Secret Struggle for the Holy Land, 1799–1917* (New York: Knopf, 1982), 89–99.

10. Price, *In Search of Temple Treasures*, 122.

11. Ibid., 171.

12. See "Tom Crotser has found the Ark of the Covenant— or has he?" *Biblical Archaeology Review*, May/June 1983, 66–67.

13. Ibid., 66–69.

14. Price, *In Search of Temple Treasures*, 151.

15. Ibid., 152–56.

CHAPTER 3

1. Bezalel Portman, *Archives from Elephantine: The Life of an Ancient Jewish Military Colony* (Los Angeles: University of California Press, Berkeley, 1968), 109, 152.

CHAPTER 5

1. Ewald Hein and Brigitte Kleidt, *Ethiopia: Christian Africa; Axum: St. Mary of Zion* (Ratingen and Wupperial: Melin-Verlag, 1999), 76.

2. David W. Phillipson, *Ancient Ethiopia. Aksum: Its Antecedents and Successors* (London: British Museum Press, 1998), 50.

3. G. W. B. Huntingford, ed., *The Periplus of the Eritrean Sea* (London: Hakluyt Society, 1980).

4. Reported in A. H. M. Jones and Elizabeth Monroe, *A History of Ethiopia* (Oxford: University Press, 1955), 32–33.

5. Hein and Kleidt, *Ethiopia: Christian Africa, Axum: St. Mary of Zion*, 75.

6. Graham Hancock, *The Sign and the Seal, Initiation* (New York: Touchstone, 1992), 21.

7. Hein and Kleidt, *Ethiopia: Christian Africa, Axum: St. Mary of Zion*, 78–79.

CHAPTER 6

1. Graham Hancock, *The Sign and the Seal* (New York: Touchstone, 1992), 196.

2. Richard Pankhurst, writing in Graham Hancock, Rickard Pankhurst, and Duncan Willetts, *Under Ethiopian Skies* (London: Editions HL, 1983), 24.

3. Hancock, *The Sign and the Seal*, 196.

4. Flavius Josephus, *Antiquities of the Jews*, Book VII, Loeb Classical Library, trans. by Ralph Marehus; ed., T. E. Page (Cambridge: Harvard University Press, 1963), l. i.

CHAPTER 8

1. Hein and Kleidt, *Ethiopia: Christian Africa, Art, Churches and Culture, Axum: St. Mary of Zion*, 75.

2. Hancock, *The Sign and the Seal*, 205–10.

3. Ibid., 211–18.

CHAPTER 9

1. Upon returning to the States, I conducted a pregame Bible study for the Washington Wizards NBA basketball team. Afterward, star power forward Chris Webber approached me to extend his appreciation. I shared a bit about my Ethiopian adventure, pulled up a pant leg and showed him my rash, then watched as he bolted backwards, refusing even to shake my hand. "Stay away! I don't want to get those cooties," he said as he rushed from the locker room.

2. Hancock, *The Sign and the Seal*, 212–13.

3. Ibid., 213.

4. Gaalyah Cornfeld, *Archaeology of the Bible Book by Book* (San Francisco: Harper and Row, 1976), 25, 118.

5. Hancock, *The Sign and the Seal*, 216.

CHAPTER 10

1. Hancock, *The Sign and the Seal*, 440.

2. *New International Dictionary of Biblical Archaeology*, s.v. "Elephantine Island."

3. Bezaleel Porten, *Archives from Elephantine: the Life of an Ancient Jewish Military Colony* (Los Angeles: University of California Press, Berkeley, 1968), 109, 152.

CHAPTER 12

1. Hancock, *The Sign and the Seal*, 115.

2. Mohamed Amin, *Spectrum Guide to Ethiopia, Lalibella: Eighth Wonder of the World* (Nairobi, Kenya: Camerapix Publishers International, 1995), 112.

CHAPTER 13

1. See Edward Ullendorff, *The Ethiopians: An Introduction to Country and People* (Oxford: University Press, 1973), 5.

2. Frederick C. Gamst, *The Qemant: A Pagan Hebraic Peasantry of Ethiopia* (New York: Holt, Reinhart & Winston, 1969), 5–6.

CHAPTER 14

1. Balthazar Tellez, *The Travels of the Jesuits in Ethiopia*, quoted in Sydney Mendelssohn, *The Jews of Africa* (London, 1920), 5.

CHAPTER 15

1. *Theological Wordbook of the Old Testament*, s.v. "mercy seat."

CHAPTER 16

1. *Vines Expository Dictionary of Old and New Testament Words*, s.v. "mercy seat."

2. As if to confirm the identity of the temple as Messiah's palace and the mercy seat in the most holy place as his throne, God gives us two more clues in his revelation to Ezekiel. First, in measuring the messianic temple (Ezek. 41:1–4), Ezekiel

moves from the holy place directly into the most holy place without encountering the veil or curtain that once separated the two chambers. This is to be expected, since Messiah's work has broken down the barrier between God and man.

Second, and most startling, in Ezekiel we hear no report of the day of atonement. It has vanished. Why? Because temporary coverings of blood at the foot of, and on, the mercy seat are no longer necessary. At that time he will have been enthroned, permanently and solely, on the merit of his own shed blood.

Chapter 17

1. C. D. Yonge, trans., *The Works of Philo: New Updated Edition,* complete and unabridged in one vol., *On the Life of Moses, vol. II* (Peabody, Mass.: Hendrickson Publishers, 1993), 499.

Chapter 22

1. Geoffrey Wigoder, ed., *The Encyclopedia of Judaism* (Jerusalem: Jerusalem Publishing House, 1989), 319.
2. J. M. Flad, *Falashas of Abyssinia* (London, 1869), 3.
3. Ibid., 548.
4. Ibid., 576.
5. Ibid., 147–48; reference: *The Falashas: The Jews of Ethiopia,* Minority Rights Group Report no. 67, London, July 1985.
6. Geoffrey Wigoder, ed., *The Encyclopedia of Judaism,* 684.
7. Ibid., 548.